Magnifient Views

and nice to live in

Kaisa Hannele Tervola

Finland, northern Europe

ISBN: 9798322353218
Imprint: Independently published

Motivation for this book

 About ten years ago I had lived a few years in Savonlinna, which is an arts oriented countryside town in eastern Finland in northern Europe, where there is a famous summer time opera happening just about every summer. I myself am originally from the capital but like arts and nature. I guess such is common in Finland. So I learned something about arts etc, and to my surprise the view from my window, which I had chosen on a moment when fascinated by Kalevala, was really stunning. So I got stuck to writing about subjects loosely connected with fine views from a window, see LearnTalents.BlogSpot.com/2018/09 , and now years later I am still in the same subject, so as I have run out of things to write about, I experiment also by having a blog straight in this subject: Magnifient views from a window and nice to live in, beneficial for skills too.

* * *

5th of April 2024   A link to a Finnish language video of the third poem of Kalevala as sung in a quite traditional way. There ought to be English subtitles available.
https://m.youtube.com/watch?v=OVuT8jdpjsU

<u>Making home magnifient looking and nice</u>

 From my blog LearnTalents.BlogSpot.com

" In this Christmas gnomes text, the advices about making indoors nice have seemed to interest readers surprisingly much. I try to collect here advices where to find some of them.

The old blog was picturesfrommyhome.blogspot.com .

Especially the earliest post at LearnTalents.BlogSpot.com/2023/09 has seemed interesting from the point of view of making indoors nice.

Was it before or after chapter 26. there were separate short texts and among them of making home nice and of Finnish celebrations.

Also after those long texts, among the later typically much shorter posts there is at least something about making indoors nice.

https://learntalents.blogspot.com/2024/01/home-nicely.html

Also earlier, in chapter 11., after 100 there are some pictures from my window etc and something about making home nice.

https://learntalents.blogspot.com/2023/12/indoors-somewhat-like-forest.html

If one starts from the beginning of the texts "Skills of Christmas gnomes", for example A21. is about making home nice, so I guess there are mant such texts along the way. See https://learntalents.blogspot.com/2018/09/gnomes-or-more-likelily-doing-things-in.html

It matters especially much that one would like the place abd district one lives in, please see https://learntalents.blogspot.com/2023/11/finding-good-place-to-live-in.html

*

I was born and raised in Helsinki, in an academically inclined environment thst valued especially nature sciences. So my childhood home was kind of scarce and I got forced to study physics snd math in the university. Later I tried to change to farming but ended up writing. In Savonlinna the main areas of life were interesting, and when I bought something, I tried to learn how the locals arranged things like curtains etc, kind of handiworks, arts, wisdom of the elderly and summer cottage life as a forefigure. But those were among my main interests there and arranging home was just a passing moment of trying such to home too, with emphazis on giving possibilitues for lufe and arts. But Savonlinna appeared more dangerous than the capital district, which was more centered on civiliced wisdom than the dangerous persons in Savonlinna. So anyway, living there for 11,5 years kind of removed much of the possibilities to go to places etc, which anyway is important in the long run.

This was the first photo, when I tried the poster of the famous painting on my wall. After that I have somehow taken pictures and written of making indoors nice, etc.

But in Espoo

*

About how I placed the famous poster (bought from the internet shop of the Ateneum Art Gallery https://ateneum.fi/en/) of the painting of a young man who can learn from the trees' wisdom. The subject was about nature contact, so I placed the poster facing somewhat toward the window. The painting is made so that children at different ages can see it from a height of their present skill level, or so like makes sense from tge point of view of learning. So I as an adult placed it somehow well so for myself, and in the impressiln took into account the furniture near by, amount of light etc. I have liked the shadows of room plants playing on the walls sometimes, so I took the picture at such a time of a sunny day. Then it was a year or some anniversary lije date from when my Japanese sputz Vaapukka seemed to have died and woken from death while st vetenarian for teeth stone removal, so I guess that some readers of my blog about that were interested in that. So I took more pictures, kind of to support ordinary life.

15th of March 2024 You get magnifient looking views if you arrange them to be in a good way central in your room, when they look magnifient in your eyes just that moment, like for example a liked hobby running well or a tree outside the window somehow fitting your sense of charm. At some later moment you can arrange something of the rest of the room so that you do not need to overemphasize some fine view or fine thing when not feeling a need for such a charm so much right then. The goal is that all the things at home would be in their own way good for life and give room for varied types of activity, refreshment, stimuli, life according to one's wishes and needed things in a nice form that makes it easy to trust civiliced wisdom in estimating how much of each.

29th of March 2024, the Friday of the Easter week

I have always had as a kind of dream or magnifient thing to sometimes try to figure out and learn, to become a great painter. It is mostly just a far away dream or fine thing, but kind of motivation to learn some things in that direction, and so sometimes when placing some nature decoration object, places of furniture, places to look out frlm the window or a poster on a wall, there is also some sense of magnifient looks and atmospheric old times things that comes along sonewhat on some side of it, since I am not so sure of such skills, I just try to learn where to find such in the daily life, without making life less healthy in spirit, less joyfully actkve in healthy ways well fitted into the society.

3rd of April 2024 **OBS!** If one wants especially stunning views, it is important that one would like the views oneself, be fond of such charm. And that the place and views would be like one's own inclination in questions oh how to live and wisdom of life. One should live according to one's wusdom of lufe and like fits the world, in a place where one's interests, skilks, values, way of life and likings support the traditional ways of living there, wisdom beneficial there and for the world. And so the things in one's home kibd of rhyme together and produce an unseen strenght that is wise in the world. As well known, arts support observing the beauty of nature, so liking arts is likely to make nature views out from the window more impressive. If there is something lacking in the atmosphere or social position, eating oneself warm with good food makes as a habit the place somehow more impressive. Sports as an interest, for example recreation outdoors with the weathers and nature, may make the views out from the windows more imprdssive and kind of strongly experienced, yet enjoyable.

A hobby or a well running liked work project mistaken for just some artifact bought without any interest in such, may look surprisingly intensive and well carrying.

"

<u>"About making home nice"</u>

" In making home nice it matters that you like the furniture, curtains and other things in your home. So it matters that you would invest time and interest in buying things that you like and need, also the needed things good for life also in what comes to coloyr symbolics and values in ways of living. What there is to buy depends a lot in which town's area you are. So if you want a nice home, moving to or at least visiting places that you like and whose ways doing and living you wantvto share, affects a lot what kind of home you get.

In the empty apartment there are different types of spaces. Likewise you need space for diffwrent major or most liked uses, and you have certain main furniture that you want to have in use. Build spaces for the different uses in ways that you like. Balance the whole with smaller things like a blanket, a small drawer etc. Likewise you can balance colours to nice, remembering curtains in this. Different types of furniture have their own ways of living. Take them knto account when building the spaces for different actions. Remember also the views from windows.

"

Green plants on a window

 Green plants may make the view much nicer and the room more comfortable to live in. Select plants suited to the amount of sunshine and sgadow on that window. Start with plants that are easiest to get to flourish. Of Finnish room plants, I think that "kirjovehka" was good since it grows so much leaves, and does not die at once, but instead a leaf or two may get dry, so one still has a chance to save it. To a dry place "mehikasvit" may be nice.

Place the green plant in a flower pot on the window on a nice moment when you have some eye for such, some wisdom of life of how you want to live there, and do not move or turn it after that, just let it be in peace, taking care that it has enough but not too much moisture. So it will adjust there, maybe grow some new leaves, and so after a few days it will look better, and the atmosphere will be better, especially in the long run. Likewise with decoration objects on the window if you like such. For example I had on the window some old piece of tree branch, an 1 euro coin with the famous Finnish composer Sibelius as it's picture's theme, some small statue like decoration object and many plants.

The upper picture from April 2019 when I had been composing and writing about the skills for a Christmas gnome like life, see LearnTalents.BlogSpot.com/2018/09 .

In the lower picture, from some earlier April, on a sunny window, if I remember right, I had given the plants one doze of nutritients, and those grew already by it some 20cm, so I haven't after that used any nutritients.

* * *

"More countryside or more green views from an apartmenthouse window"

" I saw in the video site www.youtube.com a picture of an old items shop selling old decorated plates etc in Paris, as if the young people grown in Paris had wished for more nature. But the countryside did not feel like the right answer, it was as if suited to some other type of people, more centered on safety, visiting towns etc. But in apartment houses if you are not at the street level but live a little bit higher with trees outside the window, maybe treetops so high that the views are green most of the year and charming, then one could furnish like one's view of countryside life, yet have sports hobbies etc near by, all the wide lufe possibilities of town, even if one furnishes somewhat grandparents like style, somewhat like hobbiest, music, clothes, handiworks, green plants, maybe pets and social life. See picturesfrommyhome.blogspot.com

*

There may be very different kind of views even from near by apartments, so such may be worth checking if you like the district.

These are my views from here where I have now lived for three years, in north-eastern Espoo at the capital district of Finland in southern Finland:

One can learn about fine views if one has a music hobby or the like, kind of atmospheric moments like coming outdoors and the weatger just fine, refreshing or otherwise suiting, lifting one's mood, and so the style of the nature fine too in such a weather. Anyway, for atmospheric moment one usually needs some variation in one's life, so one can start things anew and notice when something suits one, what is good for what. And so one picks things that one likes, like a nice place to sit in. And so one can change one's life toward better as one learns new such improvements, things fitting obeself and skills for life, knowledge too. Starting fresh makes it possible to reach for better quality, and so also make better lufe chouces in the long run.

Anyway, one takes the photos on such atmospheric moments, to learn about such charm, to reach something like such again even though usually in a different form, like a different weather and a different view for example.

It is a foggy day today.

About the magnifient looks of trees

From my blog LearnTalents2.BlogSpot.com :

" Old fully healthy trees often have more stunning looks than very young trees. But such typically needs that the tree has had enough room to grow branches balancedly on every side of it.

The climate, culture and area that you are tuned to, whose wisdom of lufe you want to cultivate and learn, determines that you propably would suit there and like such a place's nature, ways, skills, wisdom of lufe etc. But in different kinds of places you are propably out of tune, kind of skriik skraak, nothing so much worth looking at kn the major currents of life or nature.   See also https://learntalents.blogspot.com/2023/11/finding-good-place-to-live-in.html

The builders of the town landscape have often also thought of there being nature there, especially trees, grasses and summer flowers. So if you look at a city landscape as a whole but consisting of pieces **miljo per miljo**, there is a way the trees roadside etc make the houses look magnifient, the whole miljo magnifient as a whole with the gardens etc too. It is often a view of life in the houses with weather skills if one folliws it and quite satisfied life as a whole if one lives there so, but it needs following civiluced wisdom.

Each tree species has it's own charm. Looking it that charm's way is often a fine experience for those who like such styles. Each tree soecies also seems to have it's own wisdom, but at least for me such impressions vary from time to another, and I cannot grasp such on purpise or again, it just existed once and the next tine something else or nothing special.

Each miljo or garden type and each nature habitat has it's own charm. If you long for such, it is fine. But some others would move to another kind of envirlnment.

Lots of sensory stimuli is good when jyst coming outdoors, but especially on hot weather such cannot last long. But anyway nice nature around usually makes lufe more pleasant, for example helps a lot recovery after a working day.

Magnifient views may connect with what one is interested in the world

 See my other new blogs ASorcerer.blogspot.com ,

And not so magnifient looks, but interesting how much a liked object in a dream like area of life can in some cases bring such life across the years. See, Gandalflikehome.blogspot.com .

So, maybe tvis subject connects also with my name association "emperor", even though it isn't any position or job, except that of a writer of these blogs, or the like: communicating wisdom needed in the wide world, see linkstomytexts.blogspot.com

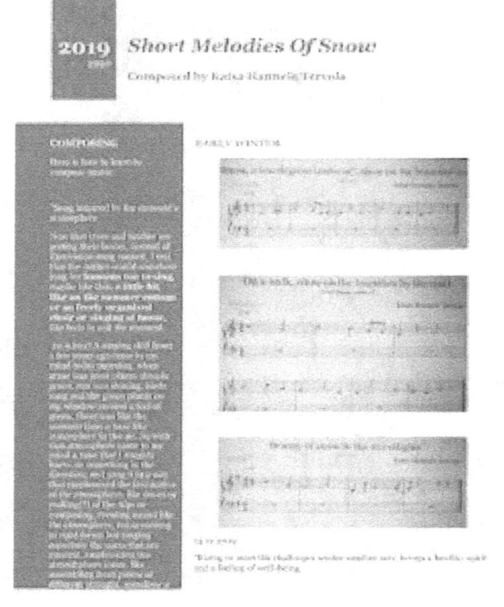

Of a fine style

 When I was a teen, we lived in a wooden house in Helsinki, and we had a not-so-tidy garden and a black miniature poodle. When the poodle was a little bit older, I trained agility with it, so we had some self-made dogs' agility competition's type obstacles in the garden. The dog was sporty and I had a view of fine skills. So the style of the dog going through agility poles or jumping over a hurdle was quite magnifient. That was maybe because I understoid about learning skills and talents, so I let tge dog do freely, in ever varying ways. And like adviced, I kept the sessilns short, stopping them at once if the dog was turning toward bored. For example if the waving between poles at some time seemed to get even, I thought the dog had list interest, so I just threw it a ball and went to other actions in the garden or for a walk or something of the kind. Lukewise a dog ought never hurt itself in any way, since such ways of doing are not good for spirts. The nature being varued around and me liking watching beauty of both the nature and of tge pet, thinking them superbly wise in their nature and talented, each in their own way, surely must have helped in some skills, and brought the whole varying beauty, but kind of place by place and not evenly.

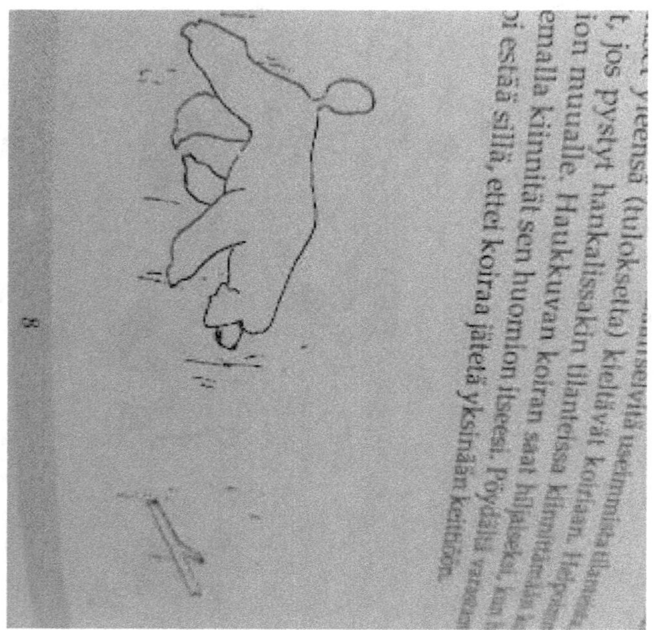

lujaa kuin se jaloistaan pääsee.

* kehu iloisen innostavasti koko ajan, jotta koira ei saa päähänsä livistää kesken matkan jonnekin muualle.
* palkitse koira esim. pallolla tai makupalalla ja laske se heti menemään. Parasta olisi, jos et ollenkaan ottaisi käsilläsi koirasta kiinni — palkitsisit vain.

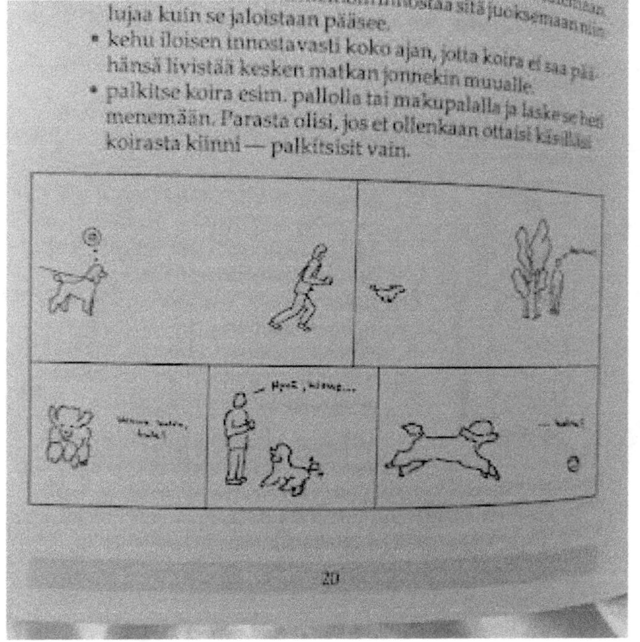

matkaa jollain
liikkeelle. Kehu koiraa heti, kun se lähtee tulem
Palkitse, kun se ehtii luoksesi. Halutessasi voi
äänellä kutsua sitä uudelleen, kun se jo on matka

- houkuttele koira tokaisin istumaan (tai nosta varov…
nan alta)
- toista käsky: "Istu!"
- kehu iloisesti
- palkinto ennen kuin koira ehtii käydä uudelleen m…

KOIRAN HUOMION KIINNITTÄMINEN

Herätä koiran huomio aina ennen kuin käsket sitä.

Koiralla pitää olla jokin syy olla kiinnostunut sinusta. Ope…
että joka kerran, kun sanot sille esim. "Katso tänne", ta…
jotakin mukavaa — se saa makupalan, leikit sen kanssa jne…
samoja sanoja aina, kun teet jotakin koiraa kiinnostavaa. Ku…
sitten koulutuksessa täytyy saada koiran huomio puoleesi…

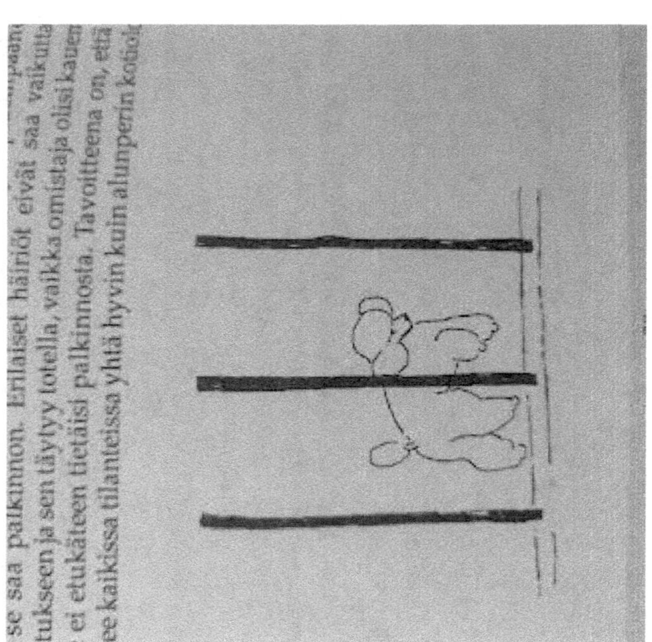

se saa palkinnon. Erilaiset häiriöt eivät saa vaikutta…
tukseen ja sen täytyy totella, vaikka omistaja olisi kauen…
ei etukäteen tietäisi palkinnosta. Tavoitteena on, että…
ee kaikissa tilanteissa yhtä hyvin kuin alunperin kotiol…

* * *

As an adult I had mainly in Savonlinna a white Japanese spitz and an apricot colour miniature poodle. I taught them for circus, but after a little bit over a half a year the training somehow got stopped and did not continue. Thr training diary in Finnish is at lukevatkoirat.blogspot.com .

The first picture is from Savonlinna. The second picture is from Espoo, taken two days before my poodle got killed, but I do not have on this mobile phone the pictures from Savonlinna.

My free book https://miraclelikenature.blogspot.com/2024/01/book-wonderful-miracle-like-beings.html

<u>"Indoors somewhat like a forest"</u>

" In Savonlinna at Kaartilantie 15B24 where there was a forest patch outside the window, and I had my two knee high companion dogs, but still did not feel fully comfortable indoors. Once my pets or mice or the luttle singing birds in the trees outside the window, said ghat they had decided to try forest like way of keeping the indoors. It went something like having ordinarily nucely tidy first. Then if I tended to read the newspaper in a certain place and put it aside near by, such was jyst a pile of leisurely tossed similar things, left on a good moment like that kind of action, not touched later, like fallen leaves. Or if I had somewhere a small carpet or an old newspaper sheltering the floir, and it at some occasion got tilted under the feet of a moving dog, it too was left as it was, since it looked nicer so. Byt if something did not feel good, it I removed and arranged the place and the room tidy and nice again. Like for example a carpet in a bunch with magnifient looks after my dogs, if it got pressed by my feet, it no longer looked magnifient, so I just straightened it and ordibarily oyt ut on the fliir.

Pictures from my home at Espoo May 2021 - February 2022

I have been sleepy. I haven't tidied for the pictures at all. I have just felt like experimenting with the camera and having pictures later to be able to remember these times. ´

But the problem with this kind of way of keeping indoors, is that if others start commanding about it, it goes just ashtray, like I have just slept and eaten and hung in the internet, and when I try to wake up, even the old good habits get prevented, and so my life is stopped and tge room a mess. I guess some want some advices in nice kind of life skills first but I have already written some 10 000 advices, so it just does not make sense anymore, I need a life of my own even if writing often continues.

My room today 15th of December 2023.

Estimating the number of my texts

The **Christmas gnomes** internet institute 1600 pieces of text, the rest of the blig, ibcluding **Knitting tips**, maybe 100 advices or more.

My **Finnish healing blog** has some 1000 entries with several additions, I do not know how many, so maybe 1800 advices

Translations seem to reflect the views of the translator, so my text about **the four seasons** is maybe 2 x 500 pieces of advice plus 200 instructions on getting warm.

Healthy ways of living 450 in Finnish and 160 in English

Changing job to **a dream job** 600 in Finnish and 50 in English

Videos, mostly text vudeos with some advice in learnibg skills, a 1 000 videos

Healing advices in English, maybe 100 or some 600 headers not so well translated

Solving **environmental questions, some 250 advices or solutions in Finnish**

Developing **thinking skills**, 100 advices to help the thinkibg course, plus a lobg blog

A 400 pages long collection book of **paradise theory,** maybe 1 000 pieces of text

I have **about 100 blogger.com blogs**. Some of them have some 200 entries, mostly inclyding some piece of advice or vuew

<u>**"Finding a good place to live in"**</u>

" In the Finnish climate of four seasons, it is clear that one cannot live the summer in the same way as winter, since the weathers are so different. One needs to have a liking for tge variatiln of the weathers and seasons to enjoy such life. Typicamly people have a liking of some country's, climate's and type of district's wisdom of life in it's ways of living, and so thry tune toward such, and may forget to or do not want to tune themselves to their present living place's weather skills, cultute, wisdom of life etc. So they would most adapt to and like living in the district whose wisdom of life they admire. So they ought to move there right away. And likewise of family members: each to the climate, country and type of environment that they enjoy are tuned to, which culture's wisdom they value. That way they themselves would be much wiser, natural and happy.

4th of January 2024   Bobby Vee : "I love you more than I can say"

"

<u>Safety</u>

About things creating safety, you can read in the long long text Skills of Christmas gnomes, see LearnTalents.BlogSpot.com/2018/09 , for example in the first text A2. Safety isn't just a question of where you live, but also do you fit there, do you like the place, it's ways of living, values, the people living there, etc. And do you like your lufw, your job, free time, social contacts, the highlights and burdens of the life there.

<u>"Home nicely"</u>

" When I in Savonlinna bought a keyboard from the music instrument shop Soitinkulma, the shopkeeper said that in order to keep it a long time, one ought to have a scarf or the like upon it when it is not played, to prevent dust, but that a scarf is so light that it tends to glide to the floor. So I put a folded blanket of the type I had bought from Espoo upon it, but I feel that such is also a good way to teach, how to keep things well and nicely. And the charm of a countryside place adds to it and one can imagine that it is easier to learn in connection with music. But so one can maybe lwarn to keep one's home well somewhat like grandparents' home. I do not know huch much the emphazis on a countryside place on such things is necessary, but it did help a lot.

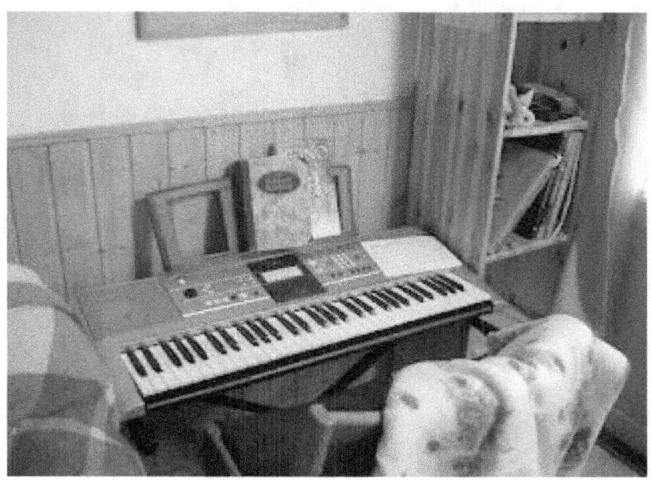

Learn to compose https://learntalents.blogspot.com/2023/09/christmas-elves.html

"

"Pictures depend on climate preferencies and on valuing such things in life"

" What one considers nice, a thing to aim at, wise often shows in which climate one would suit, enjoy lufe there and consider it wise in a good way and with wisdom of lufe that suits oneself. The cold and cool weathers are good for looking a lot and for looking with the sense of beauty along. So people inclined to such life all the time tend to produce beautiful pictures with lots of details. So if you like some other type of pictures, for example with less details and more social, that is typically a question of climate preferences, of to where you would suit. There are such pictures too, but one ought to searvh for them in connection with cultural traditions of that climate, kind of see the ways of living as wholes. Likewise the emphazies on different areas of life are climate and culture dependent.

These texts of mine are on a general level just to allow local variation. So ghe pictures are usually much more local, and they depend on me having liked those areas of lufe and so having treated the artifacts well and with good spirit, kind of feeling them kind of precious to me, as parts of the thinfs in my lufe which I had myself chosen.

"

"

g17. Fair play keeps things well for life in the living environment.
"

"

66. Sparklingly fascinating human relationships
If one is one's true self in one's human relationships, in one's everyday life encounters, the others too have their characteristics. So if one goies along with them somewhat, the amount like most fascuinates in each type of characteristic, always only for a few minutes or like feels best for onself and is natural. Then one can from one's human cantact each one learn something about life, even if one were different from the other one and even if the others were not so wise and fascinating ordinarily.
So one learns about life, lives a fascinating everuday life, and from each person one can choose which characteristics are like what I am interested in and which get löeft further away. In this way one sometimes gets sparklingly fascinating human relationships, but that means that one should not be rigid, formal or lie to oneself.

67. With things it is the same: if you can yourself choose the distance and how much you associate with them, things are much more fascinating.
"

<u>My books</u>

My books, booklets and ebooks are for sale at the Amazon internet bookshops. Most of them you can find at www.amazon.com/author/khtervola .

At my blog MiracleLikeNature.BlogSpot.com there are blog links and free download links for quite many of my books.

My old blog about making indoors nice

 I guess my old blog https://picturesfrommyhome.blogspot.com contains many advices which the readers of this blog are searching for. In addition there is my Christmas gnome skills blog LearnTalents.BlogSpot.com .

You might be interested in reading the back cover texts of my books of the Christmas gnome/elf skills series, by clicking the headers at

https://www.amazon.com/dp/B0BLLS8BWC?binding=kindle_edition&ref_=ast_author_bsi

Or start reading from the beginnkng of tge first book at

LearnTalents.BlogSpot.com/2018/09

These ought to bring many skills useful in creating a home that is nice to live in.

A wished for feeling of richness connects with succeeding in buying, and not with wasting money against feelings

" A wished for feeling of richness connects with succeeding in buying, and not with wasting money against feelings

 A wished for feeling of richness often connects with someone having bought something that they like and which kind of suits them so well that it lifts their life on that area of life more than similar things bought without skills in choosing. It also connects with the liked cloth or whatever being kept well.

Choising right in buying connects with choosing right product based on the colour symbolics, style snd product logo or tge like associations about what extra good sides the oroduct ought to have, to which kind of way of life it is intended, supposing that it is for a large group, for example all youbg men type of values who value blye kind of view. If one sometimes needs more room for feelings, one sometimes buys red.

Suomeksi asiakkaanavain.blogspot.com

"

From my blog LearnTalents.BlogSpot.com

See also MiracleLikeNature.Blogspot.com

<u>Heating a room by ventilating quickly the air dry</u>

" " A66. In the old times people spent lots of time outdoors, so propably they did not feel so cold indoors either. If it is cool and moist indoors but quite much colder outdoors, then even if it is raining, **open a window and ventilate quickly a quite big part of the room's air** and while doing that keep woolen socks on feet and a blanket around your feet, a woolen shirt on too, and then shut the wo´indows etc and keep the blanket etc and **let the warm air near the roof of the room warm quickly the new cold and so much more dry air in the room** and **so in a few minutes you can have a warm room**. "

I.e. open a quite big window or an outdoor, and go to the muddle of the room and sense the air there. When there comes a feeling that the air starts to feel completely dry, go quickly to close the window or door. Wait a minute or two for the room air to get warm as if there had been a heater on too strong.

"

From my blog learntalents.blogspot.com

See https://learntalents.blogspot.com/2024/01/warm-winter-clothes.html

<u>Grandparents' home</u>

" a17. I do not have children, but I guess that grandparents' home is made nice for the elderly couple. They reserve room for hobbies, and arrange home so that it would be good for the work like and needed things done, nice and handy, and offer support for feelings if there is a need to help someone. So things are ok from school like thinking's view and from tge point of view of daily lufe, but rise to the level of arts, wisdom of life and maybe compare to high culture. The skills for this come from experience : I know this well, so I do this in a way that is good quality and good life. So, like a mosaic of different things done in life, the interior finds it's shape as the sum of things done, some visual eye with wisdom of lufe and knowledge of what is generally good for things done and for wisdom of lufe, playing their essential part kn it.

" learntalents.blogspot.com

24.9.2023 My new book https://www.amazon.com/Wisdom-Christmas-Elves-Hannele-Tervola-ebook/dp/B0CJMBD43W?ref_=ast_author_dp has something about making home nice and magnifient looking, but maybe half of that is quoted from this blog.

14.1.2024 https://learntalents.blogspot.com/2024/01/home-nicely.html

Live next to fascinating places

It is quite harmonious if you and your neighbours agree about values and ways of living in the miljo, like if you almost all have come to live in the town based on it's attractions and to the district based on the way of life it offers.

<u>About making indoors nice</u>

" L26. In Savonlinna there was via the medieval Olavinlinna castle and the town's name a liking of many of the licals for the castle theme, for what is good in it, like for example fine views out of the window or balcony, nsture around with something skilled and stylish build too, and this united with handicrafts, natural materials, comfortable living, living the weathers, etc, so that there was a such style, such liking in homes etc too. And so if it is ok from the point of view of the lical culture and viviluced ciews one can take some theme that one likes or some good side and have it along, even quite central in how one arranges home, for example get room for orfinary muvh liked hobbies this way, and then it is just how yoyr family luves, what kind of home you have, what is it good for, how is it pleadant and easy to take care of.

L27. Typically houses and other town views look magnifient when looked together with the trees in front of them, but if there is no trees near them they look like nothing special, not so good for living. But one can observe the views in several ways, not all magnifient. So looking in a beautiful wsy is a skill which makes life much more comfortable. "

From my lobg blog text Skills of Christmas gnomes learntalents.blogspot.com

Tuesday, January 12, 2021

<u>About renting or selling an apartment</u>

 The town I live in, Savonlinna in eastern Finland in North-East Europe, is a tourist town with summer time important in that, and the area has lots of summer cottages too. So the area is somewhat specialiced to renting and selling apartment successfully, to satisfied buyers. One key to that success is that the area has well liked major attractions and major professions, and so the fascination of the place comes largely from them, and so from their point of view there are some clear human types that like to come, and some others who do not like would maybe like to travel to some other famous district and the available travel etc advertisements offer those to them (but those are not found here or in connection with this district but instead on for example in connection with the internet sites of similar interests as those places' highlights and attractions). But so of each person seeking for an apartment the olderpeople in the district know which type of person it is and so what kinds of apartment and living environment he/she would like. And so they also have skilled professionals specialiced to those highlights of the district. And so they have apartments availableat least something for each group, or the idea seems to be so, and by asking one maybe finds fmore such. The place is quite small, so the price level is lower than in bigger places, and since the locel workerts like the same highlights, they wish for quality in them and so such is available. But this is just my impression, not knowledge.

About moving to an apartment

 For the elderly moving to a new apartment can be difficult, and as young one maybe does not find so good way to live in a new apartment, since one does not have experience in suych. I guess that an apartment ought to be chosen according to one's dream of a way of life that could be possible in such an apartment in such a place, but often it is not enough that it might be possible because of facts,but instead one ought to estimate it like a product in a shop: what does it's style say, what does it's style say it offers and which way of life is it then, can you live approximately so and be happy, without being very far from such ways? Like if some place is quiet life, maybe they do not like sporty life there even if it looks possible in questions of distances to places etc. On the other hand, if there are good sides in the apartment that you choose, they do not need to determine the whole picture of how you live there, but instead you can have all your life and just in addition some of those good sides too, via which you maybe find a common tune with some neighbours. If you like the apartment's way of life and it's good sides somewhat like a product you would want to buiy in a shop, like the life they offer, in the form that they offer but with some individual freedom too, then living such a life, in ways natural to you, especially in what affects others, especially as is seen or noticed by all,creates a place to live there, even if you are used to some other kinds of life with some other common tunes,common values. Then just taking care that you have enough freedom and possibilities of choices in your daily life, without needing to give up major safety & place to live in, gives you a new home for long term too there, as far as I know.

18.1.2021 Originally, when a house was build, it was often planned so that there was some theme or a bunch of themes according to the street name and what it brings to mind, and according to the number of the apartment, so that the inhabitant would have some good version of such things if she/he was a model of such to others because of the name & number. So it is also possible to choose what type of apartmet one lives in so that the number symbolics and what the street name brings to mind are along the same lines, something that one could have come to choose by oneself. But often when there have been repairwork or apartmets united or new formed, the numbers have changed and sometimes rarely the street name too. Likewise there may come changis in things like whether there is a retaurant or a shop near by, what activities there are possible etc, so that these do not always go right, but I guess that there is somne more ca´harm in a place where they go right. If one wants to know what the numbers of the apartments originally were, one could ask from a shop that sells with good quality things whose style tells about their possible uses, like for example a good quality big supermarket.

Monday, June 29, 2020

Pets are magnifient

I have always liked animals, because I value healthy natural life, nature, weathers, sports and gesture language. I also think that animals are wise and I like the way they express emotions. I also think that many animals are beautiful in a kind of atmospheric way. When there is an ordinary day of work or studies, a pet can bring to it a taste of another kind of world, another kind of way of living the daily life, and can be more magnifient looking than one tired from work or studies. But pets demand lots of attention and lots of daily care for all the years one has them. The easiest are maybe aquarium fishes, then mice or the like. Dogs and cats demand lots of attention, a way of life suited to them. There are many breeds if dogs. The best choice is a breed you love and admire, like for example a sporty arctic dog for some, or a conversating wise dwarf dog for many of the elderly.

My poodle Banjo some years ago. The poodle's coat demands much care. Poodle is a typical dog breed for those who would like to be hair dressers by their profession.

Sunday, June 28, 2020

Melodies about harmony

This is a harmony of a choir singing some familiar song, it's harmony from which one canlearn to live in harmony. It's for many people from many continents in Europe or in connection with Europen culture.
 (I came to think of it in connection with the Eurovision song contest. The four parts of equal lenght are: 1. theory, 2. practice, 3. ideals and 4. collecting them all together to living teh daily life.)

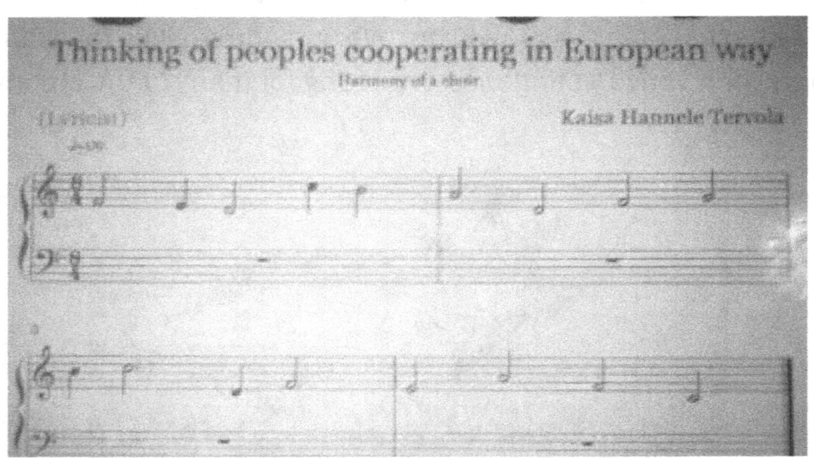

This second one is the same for birds in the trees:

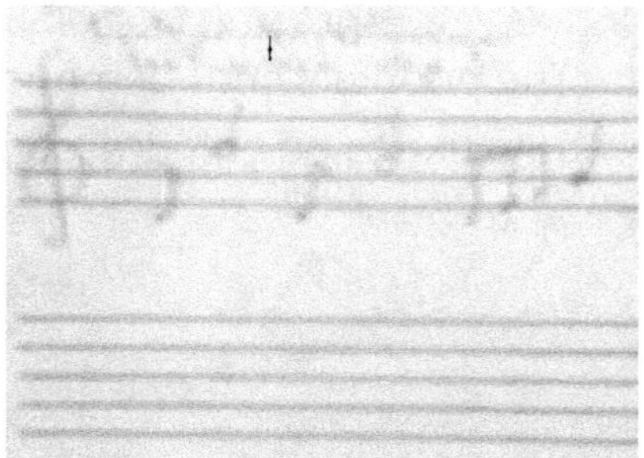

This is an old melody of mine about finding how people support from their heart a good future for the world, for the present and future generations:

This is a some kind of attempt at harmony like in this summer time opera festivalt own Savonlinna that I live in:

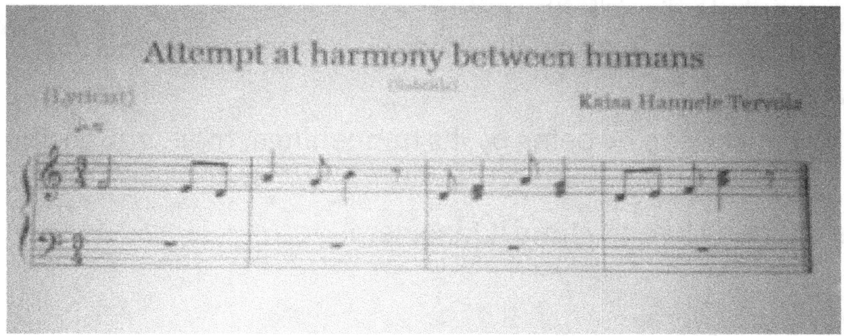

My melodies https://composingmelodies.blogspot.com
About moral http://healthilymoral.blogspot.com

Wednesday, June 24, 2020

<u>Luxory feeling at home</u>

The following can give a luxory feeling to a home:
 1) The skills of succeeding in shopping: buy only one thing at a time and pay attention to the styles of the packeges and choose by them according to what is your dream about way of life.
 2) One room per adult inhabitant brings a luxory feeling to a home
 3/ Money tree plant
 4) The cooking tips of this blog
 5) Music, I guess that especially the radio
 6) Warm enough: blankets and woolen socks
 7) The colour of your computer, symbolic colours of other things too
 8) My blog To a dream job
 9) The town you live in chosen by being by it's happenings, main professions and culture one that you like a lot
 10) Spend with each thing just the time it fascinates you.

* * *

""<u>Coxy indoors</u>

Just an attempt, a not so good day for me. Last part watching nature outdoors. In parenthesis the keyboard.

"

 Seeks to be something like having bought something but the fascination staying for a long time. Picking nice things to be centers of attention and content to life, like listening to music. Here in a picture from a year ago <u>my favourite poems</u> borrowed from library.

And I meant finding peace for one'sliving even if there are factors disturbing the atmosphere, like today is 75 years from the end of World War II.
"

 From the third part of my gnome skills text Tale like fascination in everyday life, Skills of Gnomes 3., Gnome like life in the modern world

https://learntalents.blogspot.com/2020/02/some-additional-remarks-about-gnome.html
"

Saturday, March 28, 2020

Room for free time and Arts

"The Nätki suburb I live in the countryside town Savonlinna in eastern Finland has a
fascination of it's own. It is much like a "Huaah!" like feeling instead of work as a burden,
like is fit for a holiday travel destination and free time. I guess that mnay would like to learn
these good sides and adopt them where they live, but not all.
* local newspaper that tells about the local highlights and no work magazines etc
* food shop that values comfortable ways and good quality fit for arts
* food helps to put work aside and brings room for free time
* religion
* music but choose instrument or CD player with a quiet sound so that you do nto disturb
neighbours
* my blog http://todreamjob.blogspot.com could bring more skills
* the weather too http://finnishskills.blogspot.com/2014/11/living-with-seasons.html is a
"Huaah!" like experience
* the advice "Live and let other live!" https://finnishskills.blogspot.com/2012/10/live-and-
let-others-live.html would help the harmony of the neighbourhood
* Lots of time at home can bring an individual way of doing suited at home, listeing the
one's own insights
* To follow the night time quietness of an apartmenthouse roguhly but allowing sounds of
living
(And maybe my blog http://picturesfrommyhome.blogspot.com)"

About learning arts

I have liked arts all my life and that is typical in Finland, at least in the capital district where I grew up. In school and in hobbies I learmed basics of them but did not learnm to do them on my own. The last ten years here in Savonlinna, in my 40's, where there is a big summer time arts happenening: Savonlinna Opera Festival in every July, I have learned something of the professional side of arts. In the capital districts I learned of insight and quality of life, kind of wisdom which longed for to be communicated via arts. So the ground eixsted beforehand and here in Savonlinna I have learned ofexpression and of the work like side of arts.
 Free time at home, own peace, interest in arts, own insight, good generalskill level, interest in painting and music too, searching for good siúbjects, the ages old language of animals and plants, wish to communicate things of value in life to the younger generations, a good understanding of how work rythms affects the quality of one's work and cultivating just quality, sincere liking of arts and of the subjects and wisdom of life that suits the audience, doing also work like parts that demand time like reserving time for certain moment that one wants to derscribe or to discerning how some part of melody goes, maybe certain note, and later one can often do such quicker, an interest in skills and wisdom of life.

Sunday, January 26, 2020

<u>About shelter</u>

Shelter like here in my home in Savonlinna, Finland, is a question of choosing the biggest factors of one's life so that they kind of shelter the kind of life I want to live, like for example what kind of job and choosing things benefical for it, and choosing other major activities in one's life so that they fit one's character, and choosing where one lives and what one buys and what one associates with so that they shelter these: are planned to give these good possibilities, like good quality equipment chosen with time and used with dedication. And then trying to find in one's life wise solutions, and living in peace with the rest of the world, even if not always with all the people one associates with. Food, religion, culture's ways and values, music, work, supported habits (hobbies) give shelter too.

3.3.2020 I somehow got stuck writing a long text about the possibilities of Christmas gnome like life in the modern world. It became largely a list of links to my other texts which are better.
 "Gnome like life in the modern world http://learntalents.blogspot.com/2018/09/gnomes-or-more-likelily-doing-things-in.html
 part 2. https://learntalents.blogspot.com/2020/01/some-observations-about-gnomes-and-like.html
 (some additional remarks https://learntalents.blogspot.com/2020/02/some-additional-remarks-about-gnome.html)"

Friday, January 3, 2020

About succeeding in shopping

 About shopping, from my text Gnome like life in the modern world
http://learntalents.blogspot.com/2018/09/gnomes-or-more-likelily-doing-things-in.html

"Making home nice according to one's likings and comfortable,maybe clothes too such is an important part of finding a pleasant way to live for just oneself. In such green plants on the window and things that one loves are important. Often a different chain of shops offers different kinds of good sides in things and has a different variety as the cheapest things to buy, so it is worth checking, for example for some single cheap thing to buy but well chosen and with regard to what kind of ways of living and skill levels & tyoes the shop aims the sold things to especially support. Some things are sold just for certain age class in the area the shop is in, and that depends on the decade: what the kids of adults interested in the local main professional interests need if there are many types of people in the kids, and so they are not necessarily for sale later when the child has grown up, so there is the time for them while they are for sale and things sold in a shop change from season to season and from year to year."

"How one buys food and artifacts from a shop matters a lot to how content one is with them. If there are for example several types of yoghurt with roughly the same price, it is good to choose for each family member the one according to her/his ideal of a way of living she/he wants to associate with so much, like berries or a lot or sugary, grandparents like or like celebration, etc so that one is more satisfied and so one feels as if with a fuller stomach and so it is possible to get back the extra cost by not needing to buy something else. Likewise when buying something else. For example computers have colour coded user friendliness features, at least this HP of mine."

"Of how wellequipment and other things bought fit into their purpose, matters a lot how much time and interest you invest on them. You should visit more than one shop to see what the shops are like and what kinds of things they offer. If you support the ways and values and skill level of the town you live in, then there ought to be some shop that sells things targeted to people like you, but it also means that you ought to buy from your own price level and according to your interests and likings while taking into account what the town's culture is like. If you buy just something, it is quite likely to go ashtray. But if you take a closer look at the material, tool or whatever it is and at the different sides and possibilities of usage of it, "oh it looks like as if it were..., coukld it be that it could be used to...", and use it according to it's spirit, while maybe ready to go to the shop again and buy something extra which needs time to catch the new ideas and adapt to the changes inplans according to what the more skilled whomanufacture the things know of good ways of doing and of using them. I guess that it could be likewise when choosing an apartment or the like."

Monday, August 26, 2019

About cleaning and tidying

"55. If at home it is just cleaned but not things nicely or just messy, it aren't as nice and bringing energy as arranging things nicely and sometimes when one has something nice to do which has a nice atmosphere then leave something of that in sight to bring nice looking, well working pleasant environment and life."
 https://finnishskills.blogspot.com/2015/11/healthy-ways-of-living.html

"Nice result of tidying & Greeb plants nicely

"In the neighbouring apartment someone moved furniture and washed the floor etc. When he left, I noticed that it had been a man. I guess a man tuidying moves furniture and vacuum cleans. That would leave a rough result without like women making things nice: for example a woolen blanket or a chair cushion and nice artifacts to make things nicer. Without moving the furniture the tidying would lack a taste of life and energy. I guess that the best result and nicest is when the same person does both.

About making things nice: do in a good mood and do not correct details so as to not to bring work like atmosphere there and spoil the atmosphere of the whole. For example spreading a blanket or a carpet."

Green plants nicely
 " plants are better looking because the place and position of each flowerhas been chosen on a good day's good moment, like on a sunny free time moment, naturally momentarily like feels good then, and then left the flower and the flower pot there without touching anything in it, without twisting a leaf, also when watering, for weeks or months, so that the flower adjusts it's position according to the light and the space it has like is good for it to grow and like looks beautiful.""
 From https://finnishskills.blogspot.com/2014/11/living-with-seasons.html

* * *

5.3.2019 If some time at home there is some place that is more difficult to clean, then the end result may depend on when you try to clean it, for example what is in your mind of social thing or things done, and so the next time the end result can be better, for example better thought of and more light, more strenght.

14. maaliskuuta 2019   My mom taught me to clean like a machine: to one place starightforwardly some kind of result while on the edged like after an explosion. I think that it is better to clean and tidy in some other way: thinking what kind of whole is this, how and why would it be good this way, why is this a good way tyo clean, and so feel better afterwards and also when tidying and cleaning.

I think that cleaning ought to be common sense like way to make places good for living and doing, somewhat like a healthy animal cares for it's feathers or fur, and so it is good for it, even magnifient to live. But then instead of a forced way ofg doing one ought to follow one's own motivation, use good ways of doing, learn for life about good ways of doing, rythm, about good practical possibilities, about differencies of ways of doing, etc. Tidying and lceaning ought not be like a square: here begins cumbersomely and one just has to do, then one h´just has to do labour, and then just ends here was it. One ought to have motivation, practical deed along it, good enough physical fitness so as to not to get squeezed because of the task, lots of common sense and enough social distance for one to do right choices, that have learned about the rest of one'slife and not stuck collapsing ones, way of doing energetic and not forcing oneself, farsighted with healthy spirit and not square like.
"

15th January 2020
 In cleaning one's home or other ordinary environment, I think it is important to not to just remove some things and leave the place unkept and nasty feeling, but instead tidy at the same time, like cleaning the floor from scrap, dust and dirt and then placing the carpet like is nice for living. And for work habits it is important to have a good mood and energy, enjoyable motion, so tat for cleaning the floor for some it is nice to be agile and clean on one's knees, changing agilely place, while for others it is nice to fing a well working equipment with with you can clean the floor standing and walking around, with calm quite pleasant motions and a good mood.

31th of January 2020
 I do not know for sure, but my impression is that methods of cleaning ought to depend on the person, since a different character does the cleaning job in different ways and so needs different equipment, soaps etc. Only if you are a good team, can you copy some of the

other person's ways and succeed, even though it may be that some equipment is good for the task while some other equipment is not. But for example which other professions you like and admire, use their ways of thinking and doing, tehir values, may affect a lot what is a good way of doing. Also, if you for example wet the floor, you as a person typically wet it another amount than some other person, and so if you want to remove the dirt, you have to wait a different time and repeat different number of tyimes with a different tecxhnique too. A good guide for good ways is your idea of what you like: you maybe like it because it works for you and your favoyurite ways of working, while some other could for example be too dangerous for your eys and skin. And so it also varies from person to person, in how big bunches and how often doing you achieve the best result: do you find giood enjoyable ways of working immediuately but tire and start crying or do your start clumsily but then find an enjoyment of doing but overdo it compared to your forces?

24th of February 2020
"Spring cleaning
When you get a spark of enthusiasm of spring, you can among other things **tidy and make things nice at hiome** so that you are along with the season with a happy mood. But in April one is usually forceless, so one has energy and good mood with which to leave things joyful mostly in March and May. It is customary to wash windows in the spring when sunshine shows the dirt in them.
In February at the spring side of winter it is good time to go through places that one hasn't had the energy to tidy for months. **In March sunny days** it is nice to clean in ordinary ways and to make places nice for spring. In April one does not tidy so much but one ought to live quite speedily and soften home in some ways by making places nice if the landscape behind the window is strenously grey. In May one already makes home nice for summer."
http://finnishskills.blogspot.com/2014/11/living-with-seasons.html
Please observe! This means enthisiasm about the spring, not about the tidying itself. Like: "It was so nice outdoors. The spring is already here! How can it be like this indoors? Wait a moment, I will tosss these aside and wash this table with a few round strokes,so that it is more like spring here in too. Now, look how much better! What if we should do this to a few other places too? If we just have the energy to it."

26th of December 2020 How one feels about cleaning and tidying, and what one's mood is, depends on what is one's approach and which moment one starts the task. If one does not care when, but just forces oneself to the task, that feels like against one's own will and so leaves a nasty feeling and a not so well working way of doing the work, which then somewhat is seen in the result too. But if one thinls that one would like to clean today,to get things nice and clean, a comfortable enviornment that is good to live in, and that one would like some practicvaö to do, like washing for example, clean water, and some motion which one would like to do in a good way, and that one would like to be active and energetic the amount that suits one's character, and so spend tome time in cleaning too. If then on soem such moment one starts the task and has enough peace for it to work out well, it leaves a nice feeling and that is somewhat seen also in the results. So one can also learn better ways of doing.

8th of January 2021   How one cleans depends on the person and on the occasion, what is cleaned and how and how long did it take and did one get how tired etc. For one to feel well abotu it, I guess that one ought not compare it much with the feelings of others, since they did in a different way, so maybe it is informative about different ways of doing but for one to feel well, one ought to know that one's sensations and feelings connect to what kind of dirt there was and how much and was there bacteria and what kind (food or what) and how one cleaned it: what came after it, washed feeling or what, and how one got tired, partly from physical labour which often makes one stronger in the long run, or from bad work habits which ought to be avoided, or from dirt or from bacteria, or from too much detergent, pr from failures, or from emotional strain. When one's feelings correspond to what one has just done and one recignizes right what sensation was caused by which factor, one feels like having done something, like getting stronger so, and maybe learning skills, and kind of more feels like with soem achievement also on the physical level.

There are small animals, insects or bacteria where one cleans or at least the atmoshpere afterwards if it isn't so good and happy, means that their living environment got disturbed, and as such is maybe that if one cleans with straight square edges, the animals etc worry and are unhappy, while if one leaves in sight at the edges the way one worked like "squaash" like this I clean, then the animals understand much better and feel better and humans too.

For cleaning to be nice the equipment ofúght to be clean, and that measn that one ought to choose such fabrics that are easy and comfortable to clean many times in a row while one cleans home.

Sunday, June 30, 2019

Moving to live in another town

If one isn't satisfied with one's life where one lives and where one maybe grew up, then one usually cannot change the area's culture and ways since they depend on the location and on which good sides it offers to those who move to live there. So what is lacking, is that one should have chosen oneself where one wants to live in, and that one ought to move to live there, in a place whose culture, ways and main professions etc one likes, is soulmates with. Then one ought not take along so much things from the old place but instead buy new ones from the place that one moves to. And so the cost of moving aren't so high, if it is just a one-way bus ticket or a couple of car journeys with someone to help to carry the things. But in the new place there are new things to take into account, also crime. And if one loves the new culture, one isn't so much satisfied with any need of journeys back to the old place. But if one needs to buy all things new then that of course costs a lot, even though it can help to adapt to the new culture, but to begin with one propably does not recognize the local options, groups of people to belong to and what obe oneslef would be like living there.

<u>**My texts aim for giving more room for happy life**</u>

I list here some links to my English texts. The aim of just about all my texts is to give more room for happy life and freedom in moral ways via good quality objective thinking.

Crime is economically disadvantageous
http://2013paradise.blogspot.com/2017/08/basics-of-my-paradise-theory.html

More room for free time according to feelings along healthy ages old ways of living in working life and studies http://workandfreetime.blogspot.fi

Useful skills of Finns http://Finnishskills.blogspot.fi

Learn good quality objective thinking http://quickerlearning.blogspot.fi

To a dream job http://todreamjob.blogspot.fi

Rationality of feelings (videos)
http://www.youtube.com/playlist?list=PL5413BA37709C0F53

Future of computers objectively (philosophy: feelings, rationality and moral for computers)
http://feelingcomputers.blogspot.com/2011/08/far-future-with-computers-what-will.html

Attempts at curing illnesses etc http://curingguesses.blogspot.com/2018/12/index-with-cure-suggestions-after-word.html (an index of 500 headers with cure suggestions in them translated plus 50 of the texts)
(Finnish language original http://parantamisesta.blogspot.fi or .com is somewhat longer.)

Gnome like life: doing things with a good spirit, tale like fascination in modern towns' everyday life http://learntalents.blogspot.com/2018/09/gnomes-or-more-likelily-doing-things-in.html

* **

27. October 2018 Many of my texts teach quite big pieces of skill, even talents. So if you read them and learn and start something new at least partly based on it and it goes quite

well or at least much better than earlier, then many others too would maybe like to hear about such texts of mine, please recommend them or at least mention, so that the option is open to many others too.

Tuesday, July 31, 2018

Contact with the nature

This where I live is of course only a town environment with some trees, but a contact with the nature can teach especially skills of living with the seasons, see my long text http://finnishskills.blogspot.com/2014/11/living-with-seasons.html , and somewhat also other skills, see this quotation of mine:

"

http://finnishskills.blogspot.com/2015/02/visiting-finnish-nature.html

" Visiting the Finnish nature
The Finnish nature is famous for it's unique fragile beauty. Also
Finland as a nation without much written history has it's roots in the
old forest dwellers who were mainly farmers and at earlier times
hunters. Most modern Finns spend a week or so of their summer holiday
on a summer cottage by a lake shore.
Finns have a different attitude toward nature than most foreigners,
because the nature here is very different from the nature say in
Central Europe, where the nature is mostly farms and gardens and parks
too. The Finnish nature is wild, not gardened, and it is praised for
it's beauty and peace, and it is scarce: there are not somany trees
and not so many dangerous animals. The maybe best way to learn to walk
in the forest is to visit a small forest patch in town or some well
kept recreation area, and pick some ordinary not-at-all-rare stone,
flowers, fallen branch, fallen autumn leaves or the like for home
decoration. If you mainly admire the nature for it's beauty, you will
walk in the forest much like the Finns do. Then you also notice where
you are going, which route you came and the like, so that you do not
get lost as easily. Finns value forests for their recreational value
and for their connection with the original ages old ways of living of
all humans close to the nature. Remember to wear warm clothes, not to
let them get wet and have extra clothes in case it gets cold. Take
always care that you know how to get away from the forest!

* * *

A quotation from my blog http://einoleinopoems.blogspot.fi . Eino
Leino is a very famous old Finnish poet, writing about the beauty of
nature and the laws governing life, and about love etc

"About the possibilities of going to the nature in other countries
Finland is sparcely populated and there are lots of forests which one
can visit. And since we live in the north and the cool and cold
weathers prevent dangerous animals from living here, and since the

wolves and bears have been hunted to a small population, visiting
forests is safe. In other countires it is not the same in most, since
there is more population, less nature, more dangerous animals and no
custom of everybody visiting a forest. But if you are intriguided by
the idea of the beauty and peace of nature, it would be good to find a
way to enjoy them at least somewhat. Gardens, trees, parks, meadows,
sea and shores, even flowers on the window offer a touch with the
nature. So do scenic spots, views out of a bus window where there is
green, farming and nature reserves. In a way it does not matter how
big spot of nature you have, you could even enjoy trying an insect's
or bird's view of the near environment which is often beautiful and
magnifient. On the other hand, the more the environment allows you to
drown into enjoying the nature, without sight of build things or human
foot-print spoiled things, the more profound your experience of peace,
harmony, health and fracturelessness is, the more profound your touch
with the ages old healthy natural ways of living on all areas of life,
the more refreshing your experience is, the more it gives energy and
serves as a holiday.
Another question is safety. Generally there are three types of safe
places: ones with so many people that it has been taken care that
there is safe, ones with nobody and no dangerous animals either and
thirdly places which do not tend to have any danger. Parks have lotrs
of people, but odd times may be dangerous Places where people live but
where there are trees, for example on the sides of the roads and
yards, may have atranquil atmosphere, one of nature's peace and
harmony some time (in the summer time?) when it is daytime but a quiet
moment or a few quiet moments. Some scenic routes offer harmony and
beauty even if there go cars by quite often, if just the views are
with a fascination: there a tiny flower by the roadside, there the
shelter of trees, there a view over the shore to a lake, there a bench
with a view, shelter and a comfortable atrmosphere. One can also visit
forest patches that are not so much wandered on, if one goes to
different places, in different times, often with company and a car of
one's own. By the sides of garden area's roads there is often tall
grass with flowers, butterflies etc, a world of it's own, very summer
like, kind of an ideal of love. And even in the winter time there is
the weather, the feeling of the elements with trees living their ages
old way of life.

* * *

5. of July 2016
From th text about the seasons
http://finnishskills.blogspot.fi/2014/11/living-with-seasons.html
"The beauty of nature is partly a question of a way of looking. One should be interested in the multitude and richness of forms and colours, of the atmosphere of plants' growth whne looked among other things along the way they have grown, the magnifient moments of bird's flight, treen looked from near, the nature from the point of view of an insect or bird where even a small branch or grass can be biggest factors of the living environment, the atmosphere of the time of tha day with it's birdsong, light coming through the leaves to a mist, how one always finds new variations slightly different details full of feeling and atmospheric for example in pine's surface and it's thick branches, in the beauty of a forest lanscape viá trees, the different atmosphere of each type of lants etc."

Also safety when one happens to meet people in lonely places is important. One question in it is paying attention to other people's sense of space: what is their home, what near environment, which are the common roads for all to travel, do they enjoy solitude or want to exchange a couple of words about the beauty of nature, etc. Another point in that is allowing people socially room to live in: http://healthilymoral.blogspot.fi/2016/06/finding-safety.html plus links from there."

* * *

Relationship to the nature is not just watching the nature. It has to do with the sense of atmospheres: recognizing the time of the day from how high the sun shines, recognizing the basic features of the nature environment like "This is typical pine forest." or lake shore with splashing waves, stony shore, tree branches by the shore. It also has to do with understanding the basic actions of how animals live and what is the style of the plant life, like an ant running, carrying, meeting other ants, watching, etc. In this sense in these basic things in life the nature offers fine forefigures in such basic skills, but it has to be the nature of your own climate and culture and not some too faraway place, even though one can learn something of such too, like of arctic nature about staying warm. But relationship to the nature also has to do with understanding nature's language: admiring the magnifient beauty of the nature landscapes and other impressive nature views, kind of absorbing what the nature is like, how high it's skill in those basic things in life, what style it lives and how it communicates to humans.

Birds are social and eager to take part in the life in the landscape around them. They may nag or tsirp and their songs are said to be akin to music, kind of original form of music and some birds sing with high skill. But like wild animals at öarge, birds live their separate life from humans, may build a nest, have offspring, live their lives in the affairs of birds, kind of symphatic, kind of beautiful and fierce, a refreshing element also in the town environment. A bird's flight is often magnifient to look at. "

https://kalevalainenglish.blogspot.com/2018/02/kalevala-and-skills-aim-of-this.html

" Kalevala and skills, the aim of this translation
- February 28, 2018
Finns have wisdom that most other nationalities lack. Part of that wisdom comes from reading Kalevala, but Kalevala is a difficult book to translate. This wisdom comes from learning via close relationship with the nature and living with the four seasons, in ever varying weathers. There is wisdom that one can learn from the challenges of one's life, wisdom about doing one's very best and learning new skills, and getting strenght to other things done from what one has so learned, so that it was not just one experience but way to learn for all of one's life.Also when one encounters something concretical and ages old, one can learn about the basic nature of humans, about the wisdom encoded in our nature, about wise ways of living, about profound ages old way to live and be social, kind of basic form of life, something which is at the core of every human deed adn fate, even in these modern times. So my intentipn has not been to translate

Kalevala as poems or fine words but only to translate some things of
what it teaches skills for life, wisdom about the human nature and
about ways to learn about life, about what is profound in the world.
But Kalevala is a long book and this is just a beginning of the ephos.

The Finnish relationship to the Finnish nature is essential in
understanding Kalevala. But of course foreigners seldom know the
Finnish nature. So I have tried to translate the nature contact in a
general level that would apply in other climates too, even if there
are less possibilites of wandering in the nature. It is a big problem
in Finland for foreigners that they tend to get a flu and it just
lasts and lasts and so they are just ill and dizzy and don't learn
anything much while in thius climate. So what they need to learn, they
ought to learn in their original climate, even if things there are
very different from Finland. The nature is of course different too,
but in this way of learning the point isn't mostly in what the animal
or plant does, except that it is ages old, but instead on it having a
varying rythm (courses twinding in a structured way), on it having
wisdom in it's ways of doing, in encoded in it's atmosphere, in it
touching our ages old nature. And on the other hand it learning,
especially at quite young age, about what it does also other skills
needed for life, like from watching beauty of nature one learns to
look at landscapes and observe a lot, understand life in the living
and gain wisdom of life.

* * *

My other texts offer suport for this endeavour: I have written about:
* living wisely the seasons
http://finnishskills.blogspot.fi/2014/11/living-with-seasons.html
* healthy ways of living and doing
http://finnishskills.blogspot.fi/2015/11/healthy-ways-of-living.html
* learning thinking skills http://pikakoulu.blogspot.fi ,
http://quickerlearning.blogspot.fi
* learning other skills http://learntalents.blogspot.fi
* working life and feelings http://workandfreetime.blogspot.fi
I have also translated some famous Finnish poems:
http://EinoLeinopoems.blogspot.fi

* * *

February 28th is the time of the year when winter skills are at their
highest, and so it is also Kalevala's day in Finland, day of the
Finnish culture.

* * *"

http://finnishskills.blogspot.com/2018/06/weathers-charm.html

"Thursday, June 7, 2018
Weathers' charm
I do not know for sure how being with the weathers, their fascination
and the reaching for the skills they need, is taught. But maybe if one
as young or beginner would go out to look at some fascinating weather,
like storm coming or storm having just passed, and just look at the
magnifient clouds, sun shining somewhere through, feel the atmosphere
of the moment with someone who understand the charm of such and has
the skills of living such weathers, for example one's papa, and at the
same time another separate thing is to be prepared for the adjustemnts
between cold and hot, moisture level changing, rain coming, sun
passing through etc, which one can learn from wild birds which do well
and from the tree species orginally from the climate one is in. So
having trees and other nature at the spot is a good side.
Similarly one can later learn about the charm of milder weathers from
those who like them, enjoy them. This is one reason why it is good to
talk of the weather: to learn skills in living, to get advices from
those who like them, them telling what is it that charms then in mild
rain sun passing through etc.
But I think it is very climate dependent what weather one should start
from and which to emphasize to find a pleasant and healthy way of
living all the weathers and moments of the day. Often more sporty
moving is good for the cooler weathers and for varying weATHERS.

By the words of a traditional Russian song (In the forest not a leaf
moves) "Even if I would forget everything else, this charming moment I
would never forget."

* * *

6. September 2018   I am not sure of this, but my impression is that each weather, also in
widely different climates, is best lived in a way which you find when you pay central
attention to some fine whole of the nature, like an atmospheric branch in nature, that is
especially spirited in it's view of how to live such wetaher and to which heights one's
wisdom of life, skill, virtues of character and enjoyment of life could so rise,for example on
some animal of the wilderness, and from siuch viewpoint pay attention to it's view on the
ways of living: that is what is the way of living such wetahers and such temperatures,
maybe such days, evenings, nights & mornings. Follow that advice and search for a new
advice when the weather is clearly different.""

Cooking tip (better tasting from the same food)

"About cooking

Translated from my blog
http://tunteetjatekemisentapa.blogspot.fi/2016/04/ruuanlaitosta.html

"Better tasting from the same food
When you cook food or estimate the amounts of it's substances, and if you have earlier cooked the same or something quite like it, then you have an emotionally felt estimate of when it is fried or with which amounts of substances, it would have been at it's best or just as certain type at it's best. And when you take to be your guidelines those emotionally felt estimates about time lenghts, cookedness, amounts of food substancies, about which elements fit well together, etc, then with the same amount of labour, time, money and foods you get better food.
Likeise if you have skills in other skills, ten rythming your actions according to emotionally felt estimates you can reac your best.""

*

Another cooking tip from my text about healthy ways of living and doing things
http://finnishskills.blogspot.fi/2015/11/healthy-ways-of-living.html

"264. If one does something in rigid ways as if work all the time, one's understanding does not develop into as good as via more complex rich ways of doing even the same work, much less than life skills at large would give. That is why it would be good to instead of a very detailedly followed single perspective, give room for a taste of life, for one to see where one is going and for skills to develop. So for example when moving food while cooking it one would not mix it to completely even but instead leave it more uneven, so as to have in sight some of how one worked, so that one can then notice that if I would have for example cooked thicker, would the taste and feel have been better, so that there is a richness of options in sight and one can see where in it would be good, so that one learns all the time new things, even if otherwise one would not have learned anything else otherwise than remembering past times and comparing to them in one's memory, but at those time maybe one needed different amount of different kind of food because od´f different things done, weather etc."

Thursday, July 26, 2018

<u>Money tree</u>

I have for some time now had a green plant called "rahapuu" which means money tree and which costed under ten euros and which is said to teach about money. I haven't learned about jobs but I have when I had had it for a few months as a green plant learned about buying things with small money so that I succeed better in what I buy. It is something like investing in buying lots of thought, especially emotions and being open to possibilities, not so fixed view of what to buy and not with any more money than before, but it brings a result as if one were much richer so. As far as I know there are different variations of the plant species,so one should buy it froma place that one likes and from a culture that one likes to follow. It isn't always available, so one should wait some time to catch the chance of buying it.

There is something luxury in the way of using what one has bought, even if one would not buy anything new but just have the same old things, kind of investing time and insight to areas of life that one loves.

3. September 2018
 I guess that the right time to buy a money tree is in the very beginning of spring winter, when it isn't so extremely cold outdoors on the way home for the plant and when there is the increasing light of the whole spring and the warmth and continuing lightness of summer so that the plant gets a good start in it's new place to grow in in your home. So I guess that the start isn't always working out if one buys it some other time of the year. At least my money tree dropped some leaves and is now smaller than when I bought it.

Tuesday, June 5, 2018

<u>Choosing an apartment</u>

When I was a young adult I thought that the world is full of options to choose from, fro example apartments, if I just don't search for some very narrow type. But I have later noticed that the living environment matters a lot. Each typeof living ought to have it's own charm and a neighbourhood that understands about just such good sides. But me myself I am of some type too. If I would very much fit into somewhere that would be a good choise, if it is like my dreams and not just what I have gotten used to, but it should be at my skill level too and at the right price level. Often choices in adult life presuppose that you have chosen from a very wide variety of options just your favourite ones, for example learned about foreign cultures and considered moving to live somewhere where you like the ways of living, thinking, values, people's character, etc, instead of sticking to something someone from your work environment or your parents recommend. So you would be in love with the town, it's culture, professions, ways, it's ways of living. And so you would there be a much more likable fellow, much more on the right road in the world for you. Sometimes something fits with what you have been recommended but is kind of square and kind of flat in atmosphere, so that is not your own choice, since you should choose something that has many good sides that you like. Sometimes you see how someone else lives and that has a charm, but you would make your own choices and that would across time lead you to a different way of living, which is better suited in some other kind of place and apartment. So if you find somegood options quite far from where you started at but are not sure if they work out for you, maybe you did not consider all the things you love: what if you would choose the place from a wider group but according to your ideals, character, skill level, dreams, etc and a suitable apartment then there: would it automatically be meant for just your type of person in those respects? If not, consider the place again, maybe ask for their recommendations about good places to visit. Sometimes some apartment appears nice but brings some kind of bad luck and/or nonworking solutions. Then it is propably chosen with too square thinking: you should learn to understan more with everyday common sense about the good sides you are looking for and about what kinds of apartments where offer such for people like you.

Wednesday, February 21, 2018

<u>Other links to my texts</u>

For those who feel too much squeezed
http://mythoughtsaboutnews.blogspot.fi/2018/02/for-too-much-squeezed-people.html

"I tanslate:
"... Would it help to move to live in another town (or village tec) that you feel in love with in your spirit and which main professions you like and it's biggest happenings too (and which intelligence and skill level is roughly the same as yours), see for example link??? Also to change profession and to change what type of person one is to one's favourite professions, to several dream type things I mean, wouldpropably help a lot, see http://todreamjob.blogspot.fi .   Otherwise I guess that the comon sense my thinking course teaches, would help, see http://quickerlearning.blogspot.fi , healthy spirit, see

http://finnishskills.blogspot.fi/2015/11/healthy-ways-of-living.html , the usefulness of free time to work http://workandfreetime.blogspot.fi and maybe the connection of feelings to the way of doing http://learntalents.blogspot.fi and supporting moral http://healthilymoral.blogspot.fi . "
The links in English:
Translating first the missing link:
" From the point of view of a human, I would say that lack of money causes forced situations to humans, propoably to farmers too, and that causes harm to both human´s and animals. ***Forced situations get fewer and less harsh if you yourself are along the main courses in life that people on that district usually hope from their life and from the functioning of the society, and which values they value, which ways of doing etc, so in other words if you are in harmony with the surrouding culture's flow that you take part in, which maybe is mainly a question of making choices according to your dreams, so that you are more sensitive to the dreams of others and consequently to where and how, to whaty and which way you get support and what you on the other hand should sensitively avoid.***"
http://todreamjob.blogspot.fi
 http://quickerlearning.blogspot.fi
http://finnishskills.blogspot.fi/2015/11/healthy-ways-of-living.html
http://workandfreetime.blogspot.fi
http://learntalents.blogspot.fi

"

* * *

5.3.2018 My translation of the beginning of Kalevala, the Finnish national ephos, a long collection of wise myth like poems formerly transmitted from mouth to mouth
http://kalevalainenglish.blogspot.fi/
 11.2.2019 The translation suits all climates and most vegetation types and seeks to teach some of the wisdom of the Finnish original.

When I was younger at the capital district, I felt that my own view of what is a nice spirit in a home or in clothes drowned under all kinds of practical details. Later in Savonlinna the things available have been more in my taste, but on the other hand I have noticed that at the capital district the way of trying, it's technique was wrong. **Instead of tidying small detail one should have attention in the spirit that one aims at having in the room, if how the room would be nice. Drown in that spirit, do things that fit well together with that**, see that view richer and as more dominant. Then place few things, or even more if it goes well, according to that spirit, for example some area of the room, or bring clothes of the beginning season's weathers, things needed in it or the like, for one to have some spirit, some element which creates pleasant being and well working spaces. Where it does not work out so well, leave things undone this time, at most taike away some thing with nasty spirit, and leave rest later, to be done according to other factors which create pleasant life to those things which are not well taken care of by for example the window with it's view, plants on the window, curains, things there, light, shadow by it or the like. If some place has poor spirit, you can search for something to replace it with, for example some nice thing, nice hobby tool, something styly found from second hand or from others or from elsewhere ideas of what would be pleasant, charming etc. So from several pieces is the pleasantness of a room formed across time and changng from season to season.

 For one to understand a person one needs to take into account social perceptions, things done etc. Looked at more widely, different things done, equipment etc need eacvh their own space to function well, and to understand the whole thing one needs to look at the whole room etc. Likewise **the different parts of the room have their own good sides and actions suited to them** and a good way of using the space there, their own spirit and the characyteristics of that part of the room, it's spirit, life there, in other words pleasantness, liveliness, well working, good moments and successful things done.

10.9.2016 I noticed also that when my window one can **at some places see green outdoors ("Oh, there are trees here") and right next to it the wall of an apartment house ("yak, it was only like this")**, I noticed that wehn I put the washed clothes drying thing's usual place so that my ordinary road of passing by it goes with beautiful vies and not at all with ugly views, it at once became more pleasant and charming.

10.2.2018 Here views from my window, all from the same window:

25.9.2016   Here **the way of arranging the room should not be stiff or acted, at all like a theater scene, at least if one spends a lot of time in the room, since such does not make one feel well, one does not get that rest and refreshment that one needs from home.** So how, if from here is a magnifient view but from some other place not, how should one choose places to sit and walk along? Reaching for looks easily falls into the trap of making a theater scene like arrangement to the room, so it isn' t agood thing to hang on, even though it can be an additional charm. Instead "here is nice to wander when there is the view outdoors, so I will place the walking route roughly here and sitting place there where it is good to sit and look out of the window" works well and one makes at the same time the choices according to the view. Generally "nice" is a good rule, since it takes many things into account and varies from situation to another.

* * *

27.9.2016 If there are as many rooms (not including kitchen) as there are people living in teh apartment (maybe half a room for kids) it brings a **luxory** like feeling instead of the melancholy of too many rooms, a little bit like the trees may bring greenery and magnifient looks.

21.11.2016 Tuotteen tekijän näkökulma **auttaa onnistumaan ostoksissa**, http://paratiisiteoria.blogspot.fi/2016/11/ostoksissa-onnistumisesta.html

* * *

11.10.2016 From my blog http://todreamjob.blogspot.fi
"10. Arrange your home under the rule of your most loved dreams, things connecting to biggest dreams on main places, other things where ever and the nastiest throw away. This way you get your phere of life immediately according to your biggest dreams, and not just according to the demands of living the veryday life, so you get those things to central role in your life which you really want to such position."

* * *

13.11.2016 Savonlinnan seudun sanomalehdestä Itä-Savosta, jota luen, oppii mm **mökkeilymäisestä sisustamisesta myös kaupunkiin**, saa ideoita, touchia, tyyliä ja oppii taiteista.

The part of the town you live in matters: near work or in free time sphere, in other words do you get rest. Is there a garden, **green**, landscapes, **life**, in other words do you get healthy stimuli. **Do you like the people there and the area's style**. Does it give to you **good possibilities for life**, for example jogging route, shops, hobbies, easy travel, parks, shores etc. Which professions are such that you want to live in the middle of such professions. All do not like the same, so best may be among the cheapest.

* * *

3.3.2017

An apoartment house home can be of many different kind inside. Like if you see trees from the window, you can choose green or park like or town like view by choosing where the areas you spend time and walk along are mainly compared to the views from the windows, you can for example take a theme from a fascinating book or from some fascinating thing in mind to cultivate in how you arrange your home. Likewise you can indoors, for example with the help of second hand things, take a theme which can give a different spirit for the room: there are clothes, green plants, pictures, soft, work oriented, rough, decorations, summer cottage life, handiworks, music, the four seasons, pleasant living, practical things, books, computer pets, etc other themes that you are interested in. And by cultivating certain themes, by keeping themin sight, at good places, handy and with good spirit, you get a home with such spirit. **But at the same time you need to be in the same way have a successfull pleasant view about the area you live in: this is a peaceful place between houses, green suburb or nice old times street view, area for families with samll kids, or the like.**

***

<u>Pictures from my home</u>

These pictures are from my home in Savonlinna which is a small town quite i the middle of nowhere, having as it's charm arts, elderly, nature, religion, handiworks, tourism, practical professions and an emphazis on trusting one's own common sense while respecting fine culture. Savonlinna is a positive alternative for bigger towns and mostly does not offer their typical jobs, since the location of the town on a couple of quite small islands between two big lake areas is not benefical site for any bigger town (it would become two towns without the fascinating castle that the place s most known for).

* * *

I do not quite know why I put these here in sight, but I guess that there are two reasons: Firstly this district that I live in, Nätki suburb in Savonlinna town in Finland in north-eastern Europe, is somehow charming and kind of magnifient in style but dangerous to visit or live in. So people maybe wanna see what the homes here are like, but I guess that mine isn't typical, but anyway it is somehow Savonlinna and Nätki style. Secondly I (= miss Kaisa Hannele Tervola, Finland, North Europe) am somehow famous thinker/writer, see http://picturesfrommyhome.blogspot.fi/2018/02/links-to-my-texts.html , and so some may wanna see what kind of influence I am to kids and young people.
I am a 46 years (born August 1971) old Finnish woman. Finland is in north-eastern Europe. I am highly educated but interested in reaching higher still in skills and intelligence & wisdom, with the help of arts, religions, nature, healthy natural life, sports, feelings, wisdom of life and an interest in caring the world at large to a good state, to a good long-term future.

Pictures from my one-room-apartment in Savonlinna, Finland, north-eastern Europe. The climate of four seasons here matters a lot! http://finnishskills.blogspot.fi/2014/11/living-with-seasons.html
Kaisa Hannele Tervola
* * *

16.9.2016
I change this to be here. It is already third (fourth) place, since to begin with I did not want to put these to internet, I just somehow did so, even though one ought not, since internet writing asks for distance or one begins to feel that it is nasty, disturbs everyday life, if it is too near one's own life.

* * *

I wrote a good pice of advice about maing home nice, see later in this blog.

* * *

28.11.2016 These pictures are from my homein Savonlinna. Savonlinna has under 30 000 inhabitants and is a countryside town in Etelä-Savo. Mikkeli town is 200km north from Helsinki and Savonlinna is 100km east from Mikkeli. In the half way there is a smaller village Juva and roughly the same amount east from Savonlinna Parikkala near the Russian border, but the nearest border crossing place is more south in Lappeenranta.
 Savonlinna isknown for it's medieval castle Olavinlinnasta, which is from the time of Swedish rule, a Swedish architect (square forms) but build by Finns (more complex views, and if I remember right, the round towers too). Nowadays in July there is in the castle afamous, fine, big opera festival. A few years ago still there was a big famous art exhibition Retretti some 30kn east from Savonlinna inPunkaharju, but it ran out of money because of the huge costs. But there has still been some art exhibition in the district that aims at such.
 Savonlinna travel http://visitsavonlinna.fi/en/

* * *

 So here some pictures from my home, but each one lives in a different way. At the time of the first puictures I had lived in Savonlinna fior seven years and last five of them in the Nätki suburb.

Letters from High Places http://lettersthatihavegotten.blogspot.fi/
(poster of a famous Finnish painting from http://www.ateneum.fi/tule-meille/museokauppa/
(oma kirjoitukseni tuosta kuuluisasta Gallen-Kallelan maalauksesta
http://harmaahapset.blogspot.fi/2016/02/kommunikaatiosta-nuorempien-kanssa.html ,
costed there 8 euros + same sum postage in Finland; about Kalevala
http://kalevalainenglish.blogspot.fi/)
The map is about the indigenous peoples of the world
The music instruments in the picture, which I play nowadays, are from Savonlinnan Soitinkulma (I gave an old good quality guitar to the instrument shop and got a beautifully sounding ukulele with 20 euros)
huonekalut enimmäkseen Espoosta kirpparilta tai halpakaupasta
The green plants mostly from Savonlinna's K-citymarket (for example the biggest palm tree

i.e. traakkipuu, was there 12,5 euros one and a half years ago, they sell them mainly in the spring winter just after the cold winter weathers are gone and temperature near zero Celcius so that one can carry the plants unharmed outdoors what there is walking distance on the way home, since the plants do not bear freezing and they cannot keep warmth, but one can cover the plant by a big plastic bag that has indoor air inside)

Eri paikkakunnilla on ihan erioloista tavaraa, vaikka periaatteessa niitä kai myydään paikkakunnalta toiselle kysynnän mukaan, niin käytännössä kumminkin asuinpaikka määrää, minkätyylisiä tavarat ja huonekalut ovat. Nojatuolini ja laatikosto ovat Helsingistä, koristehyllyköt, tuolit (muttei sirkuspallit), radio ja kukkaviltti Espoosta, Savonlinnasta ompelukone, telkku, jalkalamput ja soittimen kuvan hyllyt sekä keittokomeron pikkupöytä. Helsingissä tavarat ym jättivät tilaa elämälle, joka soi tunnelmallisena yhteisön viisauden kantamana, mutta samalla jostain tuli elämänkielteinen urautuma, mikä lie jöö, joka pilasi elämän. Espoossa taas oli kaikki kivasti mutta sanoi samalla kkrraaahhhh ja oli liian hidastahtista. Savonlinnassa tyyli on mukavuudenhaluinen ja magnifient kai oopperan ja mökkeilyn myötä, mutta loppujen lopuksi jää aina miettimään, onko ruoka liian suurella painotuksella ihan vain typeryyttään. (Savonlinna lienee niitä paikkakuntia, joilla ihmiset käyvät shoppailemassa kauempaakin, jos tyylistä pitävät, esim. joku helsinkiläinen tuttu oli aikanaan käynyt päivämatkalla Savonlinnassa vaate- ym ostoksilla, muistelen. Se on kai yksi matkailu- ja taidepaikkakunnan vetonauloista. Mutta yöpyminen on eri juttu, kun täällä Savonlinnassa on vaikuttanut vaaralliselta. I guess that Savonlinna is oneof those places to which people come to shop from other towns sometimes, if they like the style.)
http://paratiisiteoria.blogspot.fi/2016/11/ostoksissa-onnistumisesta.html
One room per inhabitant is luxory but more rooms makes one melancholic. To one room fit just best things and oe needs to throw away nasty things since there isn't any room for them.

(Koiran takana pahvilaatikoita sirkustarvikehyllyssä.)

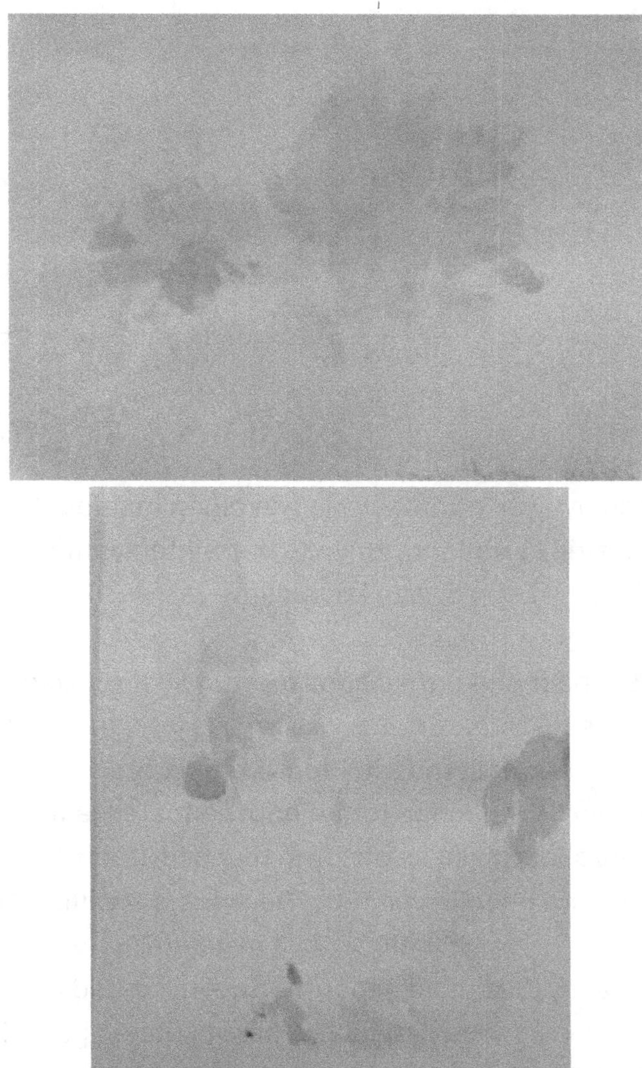

Maalaus seinällä oli jotenkin rankka,lieneekö aiheensa vuoksi vai koska oli niin näkyvällä paikalla.
Vaihdoin seinälle omat vesivärimaalaukseni sieltä onnistuneimmasta päästä.
http://akvarelliblogini.blogspot.fi

(Puunvärinen hylly on nuottihylly ja valkoinen maalaustarvikkeille.)
Olen tässä elellyt pieni alue kerrallaan, kun niin on vaihtelevampaa ja siis viihtyisämpää olla kotosalla.
http://musiikkipaivakirja.blogspot.fi
Kalevala syvällisenä monikerroksisena luettuna (kirjoitukseni Kalevalasta
http://paratiisiteoria.blogspot.fi/2016/09/kalevalasta.html) tuo tuollaista tiedostavuutta, samoin taiteet, luonto ja uskonto.
Puinen hevosen rintakuva Savonlinnan torilta puuveistosten ja tuohirasioiden myyjältä, sain alennuksessa 15 eurolla, vaikka se on kovin hieno ja ilmeikäs, kai liotetusta pinnalta hiukan kuivuneesta puusta taidolla veistetty. Se ei tosin tavallisesti ole pöydällä vaan paikallaan CD-hyllyn päällä.
Cultural influencies: Finland, Brazil and of course Savonlina and the capital district (where I am originally from) in Finland especially, plus ukulele / paradise islands. My characyeristic is that I have a good rational head along all the time in everything, which has led to me writing a lot.
Tyylilajiin vaikuttaa myös eräopaskurssi ja maalaaminen sekä aiempi liikuntaharrastus. Ikkunanäkymiä tuossa kuvituksena
http://opisuomalaisuus.blogspot.fi/2014/02/vuodenkierto-ja-henkinen-hyvinvointi.html
(eivät ole niin näyttäviä vaan yritin siihen kuvata sellaista, mikä olisi aika tavallista monessa paikassa, joten lukekaapa tuo sisustusohje, se tuo puihin näyttävyyttä, vaikka teillä olisi puita vähemmän! **sisustusohje**
http://tunteetjatekemisentapa.blogspot.fi/2015/08/sisustamisesta-yms.html)
Tämä on Savonlinnan Nätkin kaupunginosassa Kaartilantie 15 B 24 (5th of August 2020, Could it be the number of the apartment, 24like Christmas Eve, why I have written at lenght about learning the skills and talents of Christmas gnomes
http://learntalents.blogspot.com) ja kolmen aika samanlaisen kerrostalon (tämä on kolmesta U:n muodossa olevasta kerrostalosta keskimmäinen) (This house and the

neighbouring house Telakkatie 2 usually have some apartments available for rent, since there are quite many nice rental apartments in these houses. In Finland suburbs typically have forerst patches but their atmosphere depends on teh district, and town centers typically have trees and parks.) välinen pihametsikkö http://savolaisuudesta.blogspot.fi/2016/06/onnistunut-pihametsikko-malliksi.html , but this is dangerous district to live and to walk in: if you are interested in the area, please read about the **danger of murders** here, asuntoja välittää www.vuokraovi.com -> Savonlinna (remember to build a good barricade to the door for evening and night, guard your foods and not to walk the dog late in the evening at all, live in harmony with the neighbourhood and Finnish culture, leave others too space to live in; nearest food shop seemed to have ´been selling spoiled food so I haven't used it, and when I lived next to it I sometimes heard gunfire from the shop in the evening, so it is also otherwise dangerous to visit, which is a problem in part of the food shops in Savonlinna). Savonlinnassa ovat kaupunginosat kukin omantyylisensä, vähän kuin ihan erityyliset paikkakunnat. In these houses the neighbours seem to behave like people with large capacity like honoured people and there are very few kids and almost not at all young adults.

5.2.2018 Nätki suburb is largely like grandparents' home. The people here are, like elderly and people with large capacity, considerate and good willing on the surface but have their tough side when needed. They are all the time skilled in the amount arts are but mostly just live in their homes here.

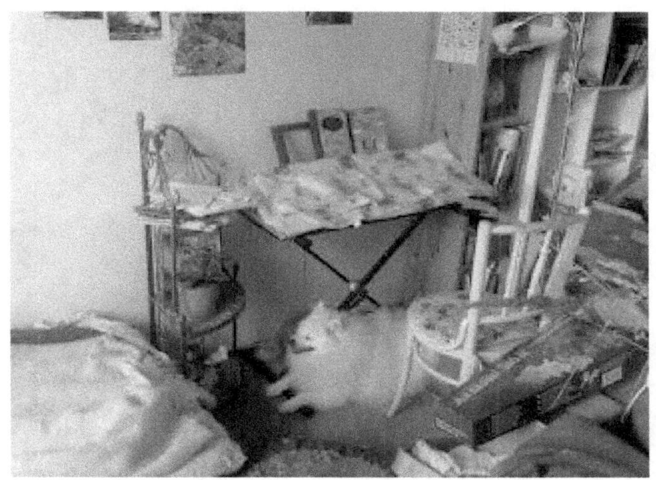

(Koristehyllykössä ja sen yläpuolella on uskonnollista esineistöä, among others a letter from the Vatican, which I got as a reply when I sent to the Pope my objective book about future pareadise http://2013paradise.blogspot.fi/2017/08/basics-of-my-paradise-theory.html .)

Sain jotkin alueet kivoiksi ja näyttäviksi, kun ajattelin siivoamista kodin laittamisena kivaksi asua.

Siivoamisesta kivemmalla tavalla http://tienraivaajat.blogspot.fi/2016/08/siivoamisesta.html .

Ehkä vähän samaan tapaan kuin saman blogin laskunmaksuohjeessa http://tienraivaajat.blogspot.fi/2016/08/laskujen-maksusta.html .

Asuinseudustani ja mummolamaisuuden luomisesta
http://savolaisuudesta.blogspot.fi/2016/03/natkilaisyydesta-ja-savonlinnalaisuudes.html

(Taiteiden oppimisesta olen kirjoittanut blogeissani: maalaamisen oppimisesta http://akvarelliblogini.blogspot.fi/2013/05/koiran-valokuvaus-ja-maalausohje.html ja **musiikista** http://musiikkipaivakirja.blogspot.fi .)

Vaikken niin ehkä osannutkaan sisustaa kaikkea hienosti, niin kokeilkaa kumminkin tuota **sisustusohjettani** http://tunteetjatekemisentapa.blogspot.fi/2015/08/sisustamisesta-yms.html ! Siinä on esim. tuo, että miten saa ikkunanäkymästä näyttävän. Ja muutenkin yritin onnistuneilta osin juuri poimia ymmärrystäni sisustamisesta siihen.

Oman tiensä löytämisestä, ikkunanäkymä esimerkkinä, kirjoitin tuollaisen http://tunteetjatekemisentapa.blogspot.fi/2017/03/miten-valitsemme-oman-tiemme.html Jos haet jotakin näkemyksellisyyttä, joka ehkä näissä kuvissa näkyy, niin luepa blogejani. Niitä on monta. Blogilistani näet nimeäni klikkaamalla.

Esim. http://tunteetjatekemisentapa.blogspot.fi

* * *

Syyskuun lopulla 2017, Kuva viime talvelta muistaakseni, tarkistin: 28.11.2016, ikkunasta oikealle, metsikön päätyä kuvassa,

* * *

3.3.2017

An apoartment house home can be of many different kind inside. Like if you see trees from the window, you can choose green or park like or town like view by choosing where the areas you spend time and walk along are mainly compared to the views from the windows, you can for example take a theme from a fascinating book or from some fascinating thing in mind to cultivate in how you arrange your home. Likewise you can indoors, for example with the help of second hand things, take a theme which can give a different spirit for the room: there are clothes, green plants, pictures, soft, work oriented, rough, decorations, summer cottage life, handiworks, music, the four seasons, pleasant living, practical things, books, computer pets, etc other themes that you are interested in. And by cultivating certain themes, by keeping themin sight, at good places, handy and with good spirit, you get a home with such spirit. But at the same time you need to be in the same way have a successfull pleasant view about the area you live in: this is a peaceful place between houses, green suburb or nice old times street view, area for families with samll kids, or the like.

* * *

13.3.2017   Luen Itä-Savoa ja MeNaisia sekä kuuntelevan vähän Radio Deitä. Lisäksi olen luontoharrastunut ja harrastan musiikkia ja olen opetellut maalaamaan. Niistä kaikista näyttäisi oppivan jotakin sisustamisesta, jotakin tenhoa. Savolainen elinympäristö tuo oman värinsä. Minulla on kaksi seurakoiraa, jotka myös vahtivat.

19. maaliskuuta 2017

Syyskuun lopulla 2017, Kuva viime keväältä

22.8.2017 I bought a new curtain which isn't so very hot in the summer time. The pictures in this were somehow better for the quality of life than those of my old brown-white autumn flower curtain, which is the reason I chose this one.

28.9.2017 Helsingissä oli minulla turhan iso kirjahylly, en kaikkia kirjoja halunnut edes joskus. Nyt viimeiset viisi vuotta on ollut tämä yksi hyllyväli jäljellä, mikä on ihan hyvä siksi, että haluan jatkaa akateemiselta taustaltani muihin aihepiireihin. Mutta paljon enemmän tulee luettua lehteä kuin kirjoja, omasta hyllystä ei melkein ollenkaan.
 Kitarasta on yksi kieli rikki, muttei ole tullut korjattua, kun soitan mieluummin ukulelea, joita minulla on kaksi.

Vaahtomuovikuutiot ovat koirien sirkustarvkkeita reilun kuuden vuoden takaa.

Vaatteita on paljon, kun en tiedä, mitä heittää pois, kun ei ole rahoja ostaa uusia tilalle. 6.10.2017 Huomasin, että soitin seinää vasten tuo elämään lättänyyttä ja saamattomuutta,toisin kuin jos näkyy puun oksia tms. Mutta ensin koetin näyttävälle kohden, mutta se oli kulkutien vieressä ja soittimella olisiollut putoamisvaara, niin siirsin sen heti pois ja takaisin entiselle paikalleen, mutta niin päin, että näkyi puu ja kerroatlon pääty sekä metsänreunaa kaukana, muttei se ollut nätti huoneessa poikittain, ja kesti aikansa ennen kuin keksin uuden paikan: keskellä huonetta pöydän ja palmujen välissä, kulkutien puolella lehtikori tms pitämässä kulkereitin kauempana, missä se on ennenkin ollut. Mutta hieno näkymä, kunpa tuo nyt sitten viisastuttaisi! I noticed that a music instrument against the wall makes life flat and not able to get things done, unlike if while playing you can see tree branches or the like.

I quote here my text from today, since there is here sometimes goblin like atmosphere,

"Goblin seems to be a different thing than earthling??, but if one does not yet know about these thungs, maybe goblins are interesting too. I guess that goblins connect to living somewhere, which brings to mind that can they be a ghost of a house repiars man, or even more likely an elderly man or even young man who is interesting in living pleasantly at home, who has been charmed by the atmosphere somewhere, which he has noticed when caught a glimpse when passing by, and he in his imaginationenjoys living in the hall of that home or goes to a cartoon box and just enjoys being there, especially the atmosphere, some kind of temptation in imagination, a source of pleasant feeling, maybe by the homaof an elderly couple, where the man thinks that they live nicely and there are wall and other parts of the apartment of which the man knows like a house repairs man, gets along with those things, has strenghts there, and then just enjoys the atmosphere like of a hand cover for touching hot kettle etc, and his wife maybe tries mostly to prevent him aand the goblin is sometimes as if insticntually perceived sklightly in sight but harmless, a little bit funny"
Koirani valittavat, että asunnossani käy joku tai joskus muutamakin ihminen, kun olen poissa: saman rapun ulkomaalainen nainen, joka ei voi kylmällä paljoa liikkua ulkona ja tarvitsee kumminkin vaihtelua, ja joskus muita, jotka haluavat tietää, miten Nätkillä tai Suomessa asutaan. Nätki on tavallaan tosi mummolamainen ja kesäisten oopperajuhlien kaupungissa taiteiden harrastamisen yleisyys tuo jotakin näyttävyyttä, omaa tenhoaan mm

taitotason kasvun myötä. Alieella vaikuttaa olevan murhia niin, ettei joka asuntoon voi mennä käymäänkään.

A piece of melody I made in October
(7. June 2018, If I remember right, the H is with an accent, kind of lenghtened and emphasized, and not a staccato.)

Composing skills for beginners: singing spring
http://talesfromforest.blogspot.fi/2017/08/singing-spring.html

Lokakuussa 2017

Joskus aikanaan Helsingissä ompelemani tilkkutäkki
(http://tunteetjatekemisentapa.blogspot.fi/2017/01/ompelemisesta.html). Olisin halunnut

puna-keltakuvioisen vihreistäkoostuvalla taustalla, mutten silloin löytänyt vihreitä kankaita kuin kaksi. Kuusikulmio on nätti, ikään kuin pyöreämpi kuin suorakulmiot, ja pidän ampiaisista.

Tuossa tuo soittimen paikka keskellä huonetta ei ole vakiintunut, mutta palmut tekevät siihen ikään kuin omaa soppea soittimelle, mutten vieläole tottuut soittelemaan tuossa paikassa, joten soittimen sijainti hienoisesti varmaakin vielä elää. Jotenkin sijaintia helpottaa, kun on siinä vieressä jotakin aika mukavaa, mm villalankoja.

Viime vuoden joulukuussa opin kutomaan kunnollista ja harrastin kutomista ehkä kuukauden verran tai kaksi, ja nyt syksyllä olen taas osan aikaa kutonut. Nyt alku sujui lupaavasti mutta sitten tyrin kuviot.

http://tunteetjatekemisentapa.blogspot.fi/2016/12/neulomisesta.html engl.

http://learntalents.blogspot.fi/2017/10/knitting-tips.html Tuossa eka lapaseni viime joulukuulta, mutten kutomisesta niin kamalasti pidä.

2.11.2017

Lumi tuli aikaisin tänä vuonna. Sulaakohan vielä, nyt on muutaman päivän ollut, kuva viime päiviltä.

 Sitä piti kirjoittamani, että minua ovat taiteilijakodit ja kesämökit tavanneet viehättää, kesämökeistä juuri taiteilijakotimaisuus ja toki käytännön elämä ikiaikaisen tapaan, että niistä var,aankin lähinnä tulee tyylivaikutetta, mutta olen oman versioni pyrkinyt tekemään, en matkimaan.

Taiteilijakodilla en tarkoita taiteellista esittävää vaan taiteille edullista ja syvälliselle viisaudelle edullista sekä käytännön toimeliaisuudelle ja tervehenkisyydelle edullista, missä luonto on yksi elementti.

Helmikuun alussa 2018

Keräsin tässä joskus kirjoituksiani ostoksissa onnistumisesta, säästäväisesti siis, yms blogiksi http://asiakkaanavain.blogspot.fi

If some think that blue isn't according to feelings so mcuh that it could connect to flowers, I must say that civilized ways are well thought of and good for life, so ghood for feelings too. And among other things the rule "Live and let others live!" http://finnishskills.blogspot.fi/2012/10/live-and-let-others-live.html brings room for feelings, but is somehow clumsily said, mostly a well working thoguht. (Here the bachground of the curtain is bluish green, brings to my mind paintings and schooled knowledge about plant species, while the flowers are white and bluish red.)

Verhoista http://eroonmasennuksesta.blogspot.fi/2017/07/verhot-ja-elamansisalto.html Kukkakuvio voi tietenkin olla vain kaunis, tunteidenmukainen tunnelmallinen luontoaihe tai koristekuvio, mutta useasti se myös osin viittaa naiseen, jonka sanotaan olevan kuin kukka. Näitä on kahta tyyppiä: on perustyyppi, henkilö, joka luo yhteisöön mahdollisuuksia tunteidenmukaiseen kauniin sivistyneen moraalin mukaiseen elämään ja elää itsekin tunteidenmukaisesti, luo siis niitä mahdollisuuksia muillekin, ja sitten on niitä muita, jotka hetkittäin tai useinkin käyttävät noita mahdollisuukisa hyväkseen mutteivät itse niitä luo, kenties vain loisivat ja käyttävät asemansa pahantekoon, mutta he eivät siis ole se, mitä kukilla tarkoitetaan, sillä, että nainen on kuin kukka, vaan heidän yhteydessään sellainen ilmaus johtuu siitä, että he yrittävät suorittaa tuon toisen naistyypin mainittuja piirteitä saadakseen tämän ansaitseman aseman, vaikkeivät itse toimi siihen asemaan sopivasti, eivät kanna riittävästi vastuuta. Jos taas yrittää siihen samaan kauniiseen suuntaan, esim. matkimalla tunteille tilaa luovaa, muttei ole kyllin taitava, niin on kai jonkinlainen kukka, ehkei ihan yhtä hehkeä eikä suorastaan kukkameri. Toki myös asiat ja aatteet voivat luoda mahdollisuuksia tunteidenmukaiseen elämään, mitä kukilla symboloida.

Muutama päivä myöhemmin päivällä ja iltapäivällä hämärän alkaessa
Siirsin tästä tekstinpätkän sisustamista koskevaan kirjoitukseeni
http://tunteetjatekemisentapa.blogspot.fi/2015/08/sisustamisesta-yms.html

My old video channel from the time I lived in Espoo http://www.youtube.com/khtervola
about a thousand videos

A list of my blogs you can find from the mainpage, by clicking the three horizontal lines and
then from the pop up window my name or picture.

20.2.2018   Spring side of winter but not yet spring, in the morning it was -20 Celcius
degrees cold but the sun shines sometimes already.

23.2.2018   Again in the morning -21Celsius butsunshine too. Cold weather goes now better and soon it willbe spring. In the picture my dog is under a ventilation window and **thinks of living in the cold**.

25.2.2018   I made some advices for too squeezed people about broadening one's possibilities inlife http://mythoughtsaboutnews.blogspot.fi/2018/02/for-too-much-squeezed-people.html

9.5.2018   I tried to make a traditional wooden bird.

The coin is Sibelius (very famous old Finnish composer) special coin 2€

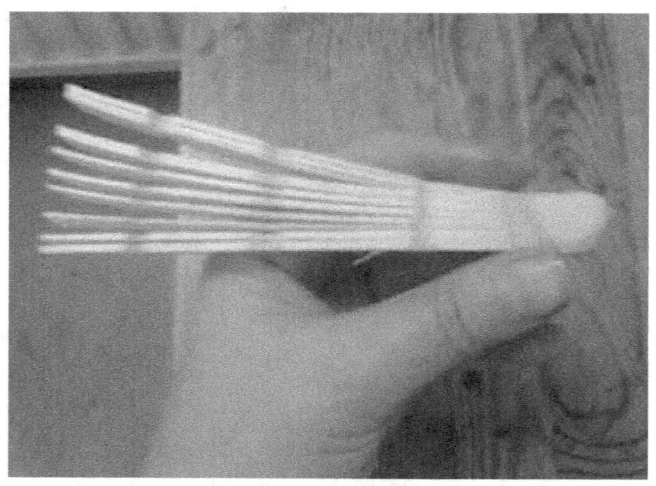

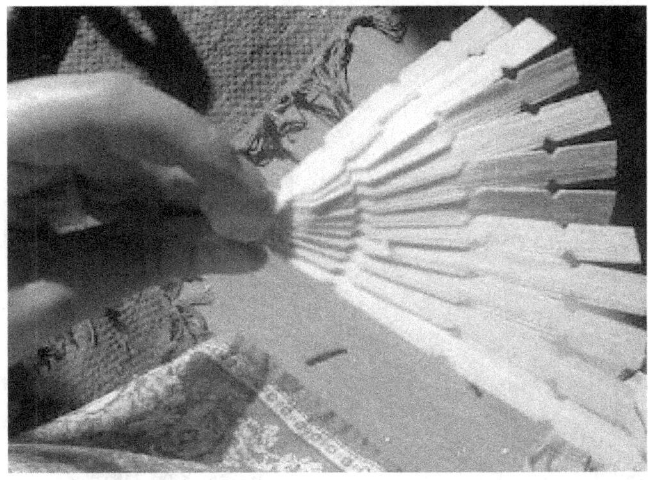

5.6.2018 About how to make such wooden birds, but the advices are in Finnish:
http://tunteetjatekemisentapa.blogspot.com/2018/05/lastulinnusta.html
 The usefulness of this kind of handiworkspresupposes the way of thinkinh taught in my
thinking course http://quickerlearning.blogspot.fi and Finnish kind of view of the world, see
the beginning of my blog http://Finnishskills.blogspot.fi , plus healthy kind of ways of doing
and living, see the long list of advices about them in the same blog
http://finnishskills.blogspot.com/2015/11/healthy-ways-of-living.html . And as always
present in Finnish traditions is a knowledge and understanding of the Finnish national
ephos Kalevala http://Kalevalainenglish.blogspot.fi (It is very important that the translator
should be a Finn, fully Finnish.) .

5th April 2019 I am making to my long text about living wisely the four seasons
http://finnishskills.blogspot.com/2014/11/living-with-seasons.html short pieces of
melodies to the spring part, since I did not find music videos that would teach the basic
skills of living the spring. Here is a piece of melody for the spring winter, for making the
landscape more interesting looking

 I composed today three short pieces of music to my text about the seasons, to it's April
part. This one is the best: the awakening vigour of life in trees when snow melts:

21.5.2019 "In the summer having made indoors nice affects one's mood a lot indoors.
I guess that it ought to be so that the summer's cool weathers feel cool and hot days hot,
so that kind of heat regulation, which at least for me means something with strong colours
like of those who like hot and bigger areas quite light and other things fitting together with it
but not so striking the eye, for example grey and brown. There ought to be not masses of
tiny things like papers at all, especially not near the window, but instead clear, not so
demanding, somehow flourishing, bringing a good mood. But I do not know this so well, but
women may often in teh summer have a not so good mood because of this, to which helps
to spend lots of time outdoors.

(The picture is from the latter half of May from my sunside apartment, which's temperatures maybe now correspond to ordinary Finnish summer temperatures.)"
http://finnishskills.blogspot.com/2014/11/living-with-seasons.html

28th of June 2019   My Japanese spitz died three weeks ago, on a hot day. He was already eleven and half years old and too fat.
 My other dog, the apricot poodle is an independent character and already ten years old, and has adaoted well, even though our daily life changed alot since the Japanese spitz kept company to us all the time and he also was not sporty at all. He also had an interest in curing and seemed skille din it http://curingguesses.blogspot.com/2018/12/index-with-cure-suggestions-after-word.html
Here is a pice of melody I composed a little bit over a week ago to help other who mourn the death of their pet. After almost two weeks it seemed good to take more distance, to wish well and to have an idealistickind of polite picture of the pet which had died.

29th June 2019 I took a picture of my poodle, some three weeks after my Japanese spitz died. My poodle slept on a pile of clothes and blankets that he had kind of rearranged.

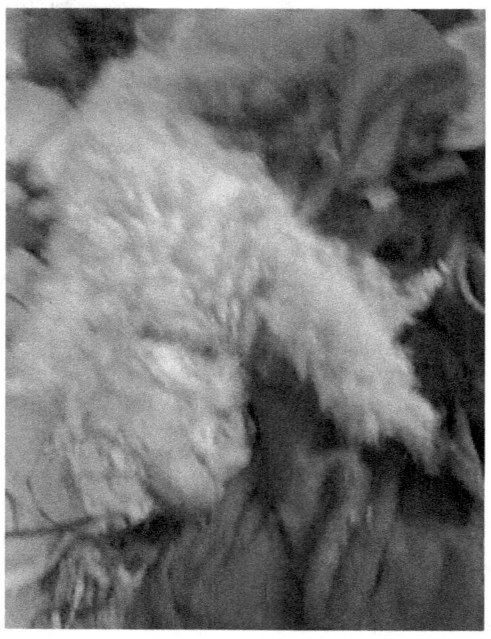

The street this house is on has an old times' army name, which is at the same time somehow good life and somehow harsh. There used to be two food shops and a bar near by, but now there is only one food shop with not so good quality food, I cannot use it, and a new bar after a long pause. But so people who live here tend to care foods well, kind of for free time and good life, for peacefulness too, and for home likedness since the district seems dangerous, and I guess that for to support the peace arts need. At least part of the people appear religious. There is nature as an element in the living environment, somewhat like admiring pet's magnifient coat or the like. The town is largely centered around the July's opera festival, but year around. Quite many of the inhabitants are old and like the district in some way. The town is largely a tourist town. All around is the lake district's nature with summer cottages too, but living here it appears dangerous.

26th of January 2020 I have been composing of winter weathers too. Last December I composed for example these (The hand written is titled Raining snow, streetlights here and there) The last one got words this year, according to what the weather brought to mind in December.

Raining tiny bits of snow, a little bit under 0C
Kaisa Hannele Tervola

Raining snow
Kaisa Hannele Tervola

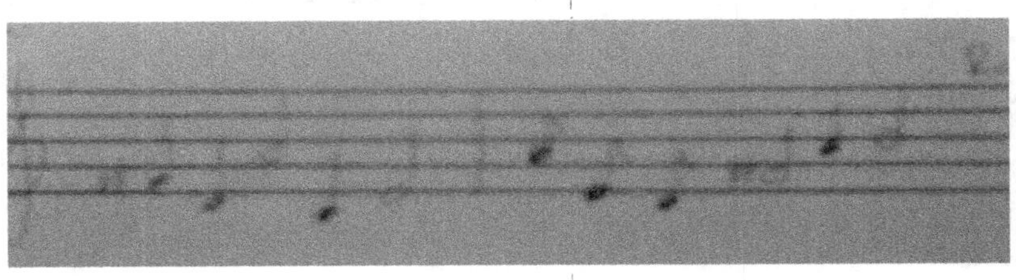

Some feeling of light on a cloudy day
Kaisa Hannele Tervola

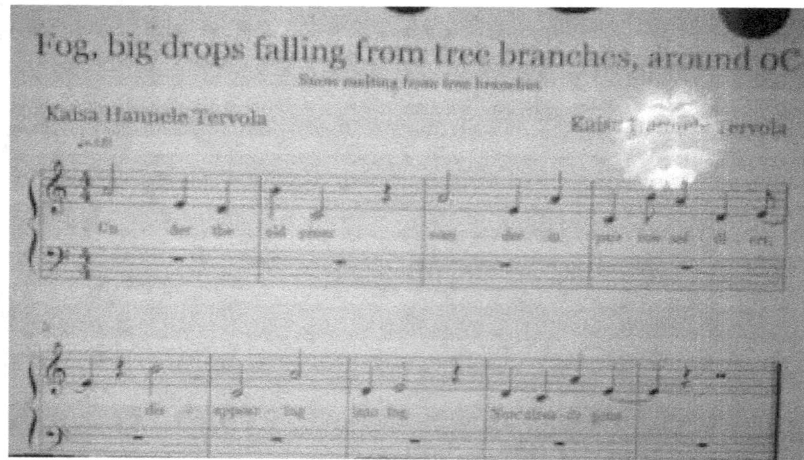

https://composingmelodies.blogspot.com/2019/09/how-composer-hears-music-in-hisher-head.html

5th of February 2020

 Me and my apricot poodle haven't been left as much in peace this autumn and winter. One reason is that we have a new neighbour that is intent on destroying peace of living, and another is that we no longer have the whote spitz that was a guard dog too and very likable character. Me and my poodle live more like in a landscape while the Japanese sputz was mostly homebound, took things to his heart but did not seem to look far, think of consequences so much. But on the other hand I have still been composing, this time about the winter weathers and there has been sapce for that, kind of a place for me in just that. And my poodle has his more intellectual social relationships and a wider area natural.

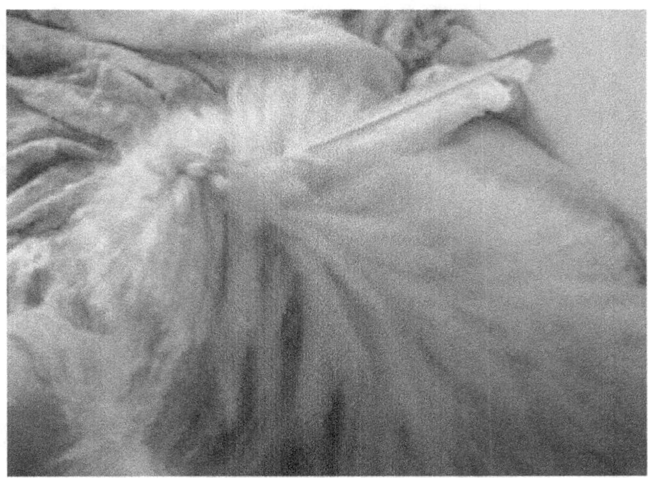

Maybe a little bit over a week ago, my poodle said he wished for a feather and an indian role of longer walks wirh nature around. So I tried an indian feather in his head, but soon took it away.

Two pictures from today. My poodle often waits long before he eats and today he had already eaten sausages.

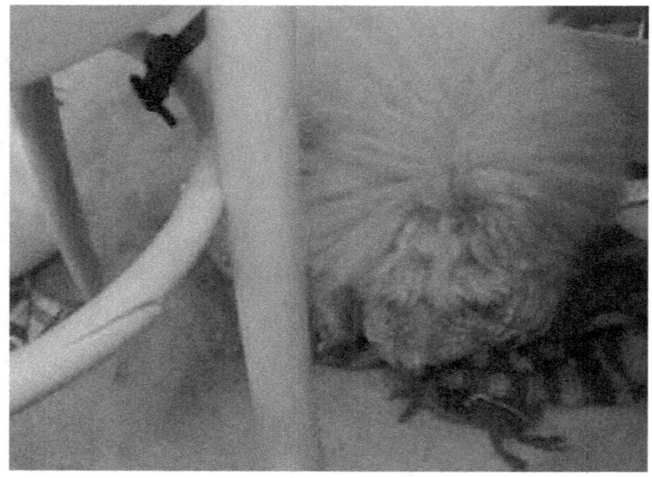

21th of February 2020   The spring seems to be early this year, but there may still be cold weathers coming.

Since last autumn Banjo has had an own blog https://villakoirabanjo.blogspot.com/
butthat caused problem of vetenarians attacking it, thinking it having too much position
but it is already 11 years old and a nice intelligent gentleman like dog. Now we are waiting
for the end of February to know for sure that there are no very cold weathers coming so that
I can clip it's coat without danger of it freezing.

19th of March 2020   A picture of just washed and trimmed Banjo from the end of February when there was no longer danger of very cold winter weathers.

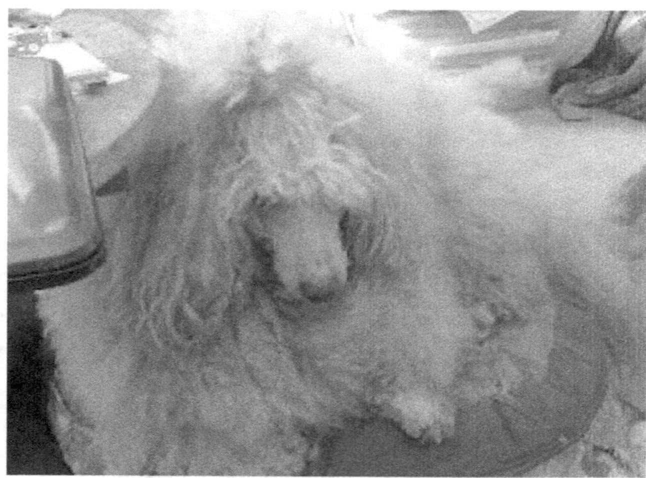

24th of March 2020   The common factor of where I live and even of the whole town is opera, much like "next block from opera" sounds like.

28th of August 2020   Before the summer I changed the place of the bed, so as to get more fresh air. This is a picture taken in the morning.

The summer was unbearably hot in my sunside apartment. Now it is already cooler and nicer.

5th of September 2020

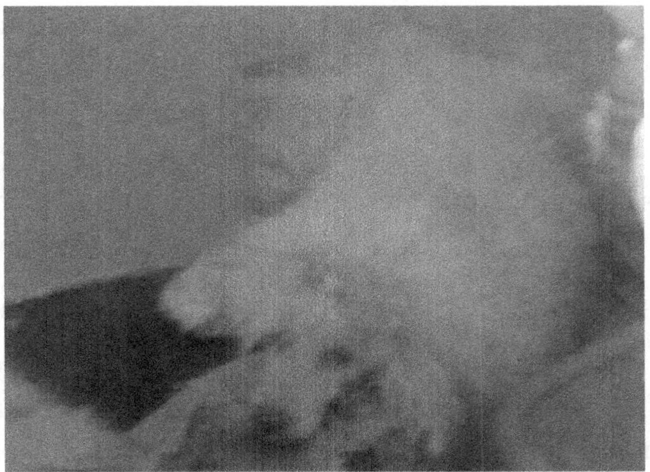

11th of December 2020

12.1.2021 The street here has an old times army name, and sometimes from outdoors in the evening one can hear bangs like sounds of different kinds of guns and sometimes it feels like someone there with agun is waiting to shoot someone seen through the window, so avoiding being shot is one thing I have giotten some practy´ ´ice in. But this is the third storey, so sitting down typically removes the danger of being shot. Likewise from outdoors there are only some places from which one could shoot in. The neighbouring house is near, so I have a curtain in the closestr window on their side, snce it isn't nice to live in an aquarium. For the first new years I cheked where there is the danger of being shot and placed my cushioned chair so that there was no danmger of being shot, and if needed I could spend the whole evening there with computer, newspaper, musical instrument, tv, etc and with the possibility to turn lights off from there. Typically when there have been bangs, I have thought it good to sit for a while so that its is bot so nice or easyto wait to shoot,and then go past the dangerous places quickly and go on with my life. But lower storeys would not ha´ve been so easy. The walls of the house are stonel like hardm and curtains matter too.

25th of January 2021   I am moving from Savonlinna to Espoo at the capital district but with a national park too. That may affect my blogging a lot.

Pictures from yesterday or so.

I moved away tuesday 26th of January 2021.

* * *

7th of April 2023, Easter Friday, in Espoo

https://learntalents.blogspot.com/2023/04/about-making-home-nice.html

An indian style shaman drum

 In the enf of Janyary or beginning of February 2021 when we, me and my 12 years old apricot poodle Banjo, had just less than a week before moved from Savonlinna to Espoo, I once woke up 4 a.m. in the morning, my poodle seeming to say that I ought to write a children's book. But I do not have children, so my poodle told the story and I wrote it down :

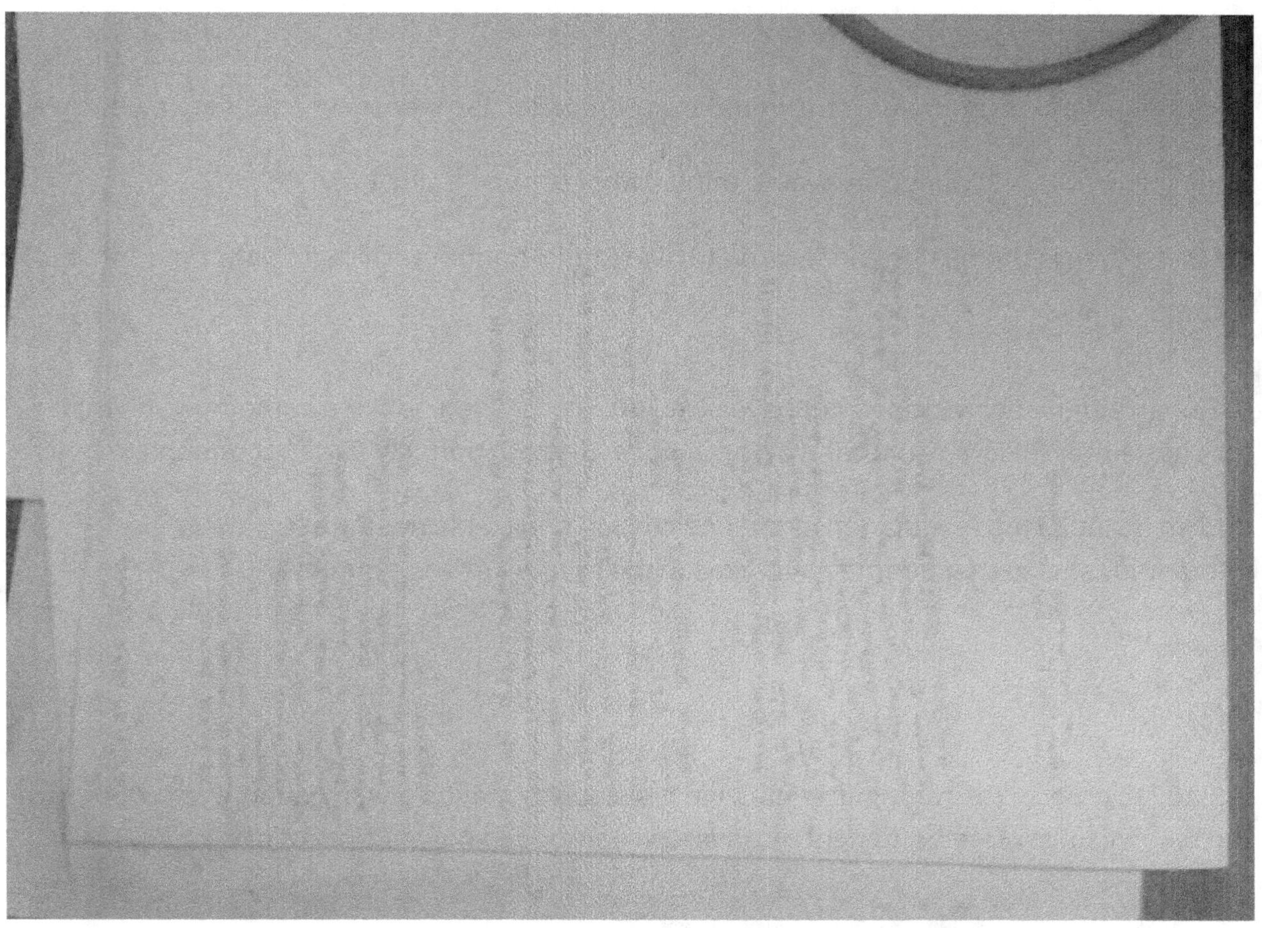

Here is my traslation of it (3rd of April 2024, over three years after my poodle was killed). The words are aimed for children, and the expressions are meant to be on a general level, wisdom of life about getting friends and being happy.

" Peetu and Old Man Rabbit

If I would have liked to give you a kiss, you would have obstructed it.

But if you had thought of me as cute, you would have said: "maybe this once".

But if you woukd have been ill, you would have rejoiced about it.

But then you would have fallen ill more, since I would have been more ill than you.

2. If you were old, you would like me.

If you would be middle-aged, you would think that such life was when you were a child.

But if you would be young, you would think, "what are you trying to do?".

So an old one is the best friend for a child, like family members living in different rooms.

3. But an elderly person does not have strenght, since when he does something, he thinks that it is either thise way or that way, and those are both boringly familuar options to him.

And so he lacks the fascination of the basic level, and so his eyes are not always interested, and so there comes mistakes in the muddle of good quality. "

* * *

2.2.2021   I saw in the morning a figure lije a big dog or maybe a wolf galloping sliwly across the tsnowy town street, and right afterwards I composed my memory of it:

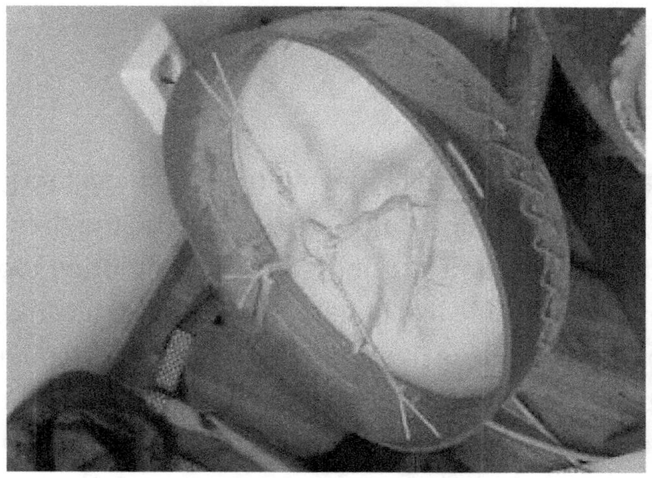

Quoted very freely from the Finnish blog villakoiraBanjo.blogspot.com of my poodle Banjo.

"About celebrations

Savonlinna was good at celebrating while the capital district isn't so good at celebrating. As far as i understand, in a celebration day there ought to be the thing celebrated, some guests, some ages old life, some time outdoors with some motion too, foods that are kind of traditional somewhat countryside like but somehow stylish like magnifient looking and tasty, and some fine pieces of culture like some song (on a CD?), poem and/or piece of tradition or history, lots of free chances to talk for a while or do something in varied groups, and an end in sight guests leaving they having the teavel or something else for ghe evening.

But this is just my impression. Home tidy, clean and nice is important too. There ought to be some nature around.
And like painting or drawing demands a moment of it's own, maybe 15 minutes with time also for the subject, for such life, and with the goal of making a fine piece of art, likewise things in the party demand some space for them at least on the part of the one who offers them, so that the atmosphere is better.
In celebrations it is a rule that one ought to behave well and be good willing, dress in clean celebration clothes too. If one does not feel like behaving so one ought to leave. Also otherwise it is ok to make just a short visit or to not to come if one wishes so. If some have come from far and cannot leave, they can go and find some quiet enough corner and read a book.
But I haven't been in such celebrations for a long time, years and years. "

From my long blog LearnTalents.BlogSpot.com about the Skills of Christmas gnomes.

My blog text "Thoughts about magic"

See https://learntalents.blogspot.com/2023/10/thoughts-about-magic.html

Skills for living with the Four Seasons

 My book "Living with the Four Seasons" in a blog post form, see
https://finnishskills.blogspot.com/2014/11/living-with-seasons.html